PERIPLUS

Pocket ARABIC Dictionary

Compiled by
Fethi Mansouri

PERIPLUS

Published by Periplus Editions (HK) Ltd.

Copyright © 2004 Periplus Editions

LCC Card No. 2003112386
ISBN: 0-7946-0183-9

Distributed by:

Asia-Pacific
Berkeley Books Pte Ltd
130 Joo Seng Road, 06-01/03
Singapore 368357
Tel: (65) 6280 1330; Fax: (65) 6280 6290
Email: inquiries@periplus.com.sg

Japan
Tuttle Publishing
Yaekari Bldg., 3F
5-4-12 Osaki, Shinagawa-ku
Tokyo 141-0032, Japan
Tel: (03) 5437 0171; Fax: (03) 5437 0755
Email: tuttle-sales@gol.com

North America, Latin America & Europe
Tuttle Publishing
Airport Industrial Park
364 Innovation Drive
North Clarendon, VT 05759-9436, USA
Tel: (802) 773 8930; Fax: (802) 7736993
Email: info@tuttlepublishing.com
www.tuttlepublishing.com

08 07 06 05 04
8 7 6 5 4 3 2 1

Printed in Singapore

Contents

Introduction

This Pocket Dictionary is an indispensable companion for visitors to any of the countries where Arabic is spoken - including Algeria, Bahrain, Egypt, Iraq, Jordan, Kuwait, Lebanon, Libya, Mauritania, Morocco, Oman, the Palestinian Occupied Territories, Qatar, Saudi Arabia, Sudan, Syria, Tunisia, United Arab Emirates and Yemen — and for anyone in the early stages of learning the language. It contains all the 3,000 or so Arabic words that are most commonly encountered in informal everyday speech.

For the sake of clarity, only the common Arabic equivalents for each English word have been given. When an English word has more than one possible meaning, with different Arabic equivalents, each meaning is listed separately, with a clear explanatory gloss. The layout is clear and accessible, with none of the abbreviations and dense nests of entries typical of many small dictionaries.

Arabic is the native language of over 250 million people, thus ranking as a world language behind only Chinese, English, Spanish and Hindi. There are many national and regional varieties of spoken Arabic, such as Egyptian, Moroccan and Lebanese, but the language presented in this dictionary is Modern Standard Arabic, understood by all Arabic speakers and used throughout the Arab world in most written and broadcast material.

Arabic script is written from right to left. It is based on eighteen different letter forms derived from the script originally used to represent the Aramaic language of ancient West Asia. In the developed Arabic script these letters vary in appearance according to their connection with the letters before and after them. Eight of the letters may be modified by marks written above or below them in order to represent sounds not occurring in Aramaic, resulting in the complete Arabic alphabet of 29 consonants and three long vowels. The three corresponding short vowels are not normally represented in Arabic writing, but may be shown in works (such as this Dictionary) aimed at foreign users of the language.

In this dictionary every Arabic word or phrase is also given in the roman alphabet (using a conventional transliterating system based largely on the symbols of the International Phonetic Association). A guide to the pronunciation of these romanized forms is given on the following pages. The words and phrases in the Arabic–English section of the dictionary are arranged in English alphabetical order using the letters of the romanized forms.

Pronunciation

The imitated pronunciation should be read as if it were English, bearing in mind that the emphatic consonants indicate more a vowel volume than a separate sound.

English	Arabic	Phonetic Description	Approximate in English
b	ب	voiced labial stop	*b* as in ***b**ad*
d	د	voiced alveolar stop	as in ***d**ad*
d	ض	emphatic voiced alveolar stop	does not exist (similar to ***D**on*)
f	ف	voiceless labio-dental fricative	as in ***f**at*
h	ه	voiceless glottal fricative	as in ***h**at*
h	ح	voiceless pharyngeal fricative	does not exist
j	ج	voiced palato-alveolar fricative	as in ***j**elly*
k	ك	voiceless velar stop	as in ***k**ick*
l	ل	alveolar lateral	as in ***l**ick*
m	م	bilabial nasal	as in ***m**ight*
n	ن	alveolar nasal	as in ***n**ight*
q	ق	uvular stop	does not exist
r	ر	alveolar trill	as in ***r**ight*
s	س	voiceless alveolar fricative	as in ***s**ight*
s	ص	emphatic voiceless alveolar fricative	does not exist (similar to ***S**ahara*)
t	ت	voiceless dental fricative	as in ***t**ight*
t	ط	emphatic voiceless alveolar stop	does not exist (similar to ***T**okyo*)
z	ز	voiced alveolar fricative	as in ***z**ebra*
z	ظ	emphatic voiced alveolar fricative	*dh* or *z* (depends on region)
‘	ء، أ	glottal stop	*a*
’	ع	voiced pharyngeal fricative	does not exist
sh	ش	voiceless palato-alveolar fricative	as in ***sh**oes*
th	ث	voiceless dental fricative	as in ***th**ree*
dh	ذ	voiced dental fricative	as in ***th**ere*
kh	خ	voiceless velar fricative	does not exist
gh	غ	voiced velar fricative	does not exist
y	ي	palatal glide	as in ***y**ellow*
w	و	bilabial approximant	as in ***w**all*

Vowels: there are three basic short vowels in Arabic and three long ones. These are

Vowel	Phonetic description	English equivalent
a	short low back vowel	as in ***A****msterdam*
aa	long low back vowel	as in ***fa****r*
i	short high front vowel	as in ***i****nside*
ii	long high front vowel	as in *cl**ea**n*
u	short high back vowel	as in ***to*** *go*
uu	long high back vowel	as in *n**oo**n*

Stressing of words

Arabic words do not have a stressed syllable in the manner that English words do. However, individual consonants can exhibit stress by means of a *shadda* (gemination) — this is represented by a duplicated consonant. For example, in the word *kassara* "to break," the duplicated *s* indicates consonantal stress as in the English name "Cassandra."

Arabic–English

A

A

aa<u>dh</u>aar آذار March
aakhar ajal آخر اجل at the latest
aa<u>kh</u>ar آخر another (same again)
aakhar آخر final
aa<u>kh</u>ir آخر last
aala آلة machine
aalaat آلات machinery
aalat an-nafi<u>kh</u> الة النفخ flute
aalat ta<u>s</u>wiir آلة تصوير camera
aamin امن safe
aamin امن secure, safe
aasif اسف sorry, to feel regretful
aasiya آسيا Asia
aa<u>th</u>aar اثار remains (historical)
abadan أبدا never
abb أب father
abya<u>d</u> أبيض white
adaat أداة appliance, electrical
adab أدب literature
af'a أفعى snake
afdal al-umniyaat أفضل الأمنيات best wishes
afdal أفضل best
afkaar أفكار thoughts
ahamm أهم main, most important
ahamm أهم major (important)
ahammiyya أهمية importance
ahl أهل parents
ahlan wa sahlan أهلا و سهلا welcome!
a<u>h</u>mar أحمر red
a<u>h</u>san أحسن better
a<u>h</u>santa أحسنت well done!
a<u>h</u>yaanan أحيانا occasionally
a<u>h</u>yaanan أحيانا sometimes
ajnabii أجنبي stranger
a<u>kh</u> أخ sibling
a<u>kh</u> أخ brother
a<u>kh</u>baar أخبار news
a<u>kh</u>iiran أخيرا finally
akiid أكيد certain, sure
akiid أكيد sure
akl ba<u>h</u>rii أكل بحري seafood
alam ألم ache
alam ألم pain
alam ألم suffering
alf ألف thousand
aliif أليف tame
amaam أمام before (in front of)
amaam أمام front: in front of
amariica امريكا America
amariikiyy اميركي American
amlas أملس even (smooth)
amn أمن peace
amr أمر matter, issue
amr أمر order (command)
amr أمر command, order
amti'a أمتعة luggage
amti'a أمتعة baggage
anaanaas أناناس pineapple
anf أنف nose
aniiq أنيق elegant
anta أنت you (male)
anta أنت you (familiar)
anti أنت you (female)
aqaarib أقارب relatives, family
aqal أقل least (smallest amount)

ARABIC–ENGLISH

A

aqal أقل less (smaller amount)
aqal أقل less, minus
arba'ata 'ashar أربعة عشر fourteen
arba'a أربعة four
arba'iin أربعين forty
ard أرض land
ardii أرضي plain (level ground)
ariika أريكة sofa, couch
arju أرجو please (request for help)
armal أرمل widower
armala أرملة widow
armala أرملة widowed
aruzz lazij أرز لزج glutinous rice
aruzz أرز rice (cooked)
aruzz أرز rice (uncooked grains)
asaas أساس base, foundation
asaas أساس basis
asaasi أساسي basic
asamm أصم deaf
asfar أصفر yellow
asghar أصغر younger brother or sister
asl أصل origin
aslii أصلي original
aslii أصلي indigenous
aswa' آسوأ worse
aswad أسود black
athaath أثاث furniture
athar أثر monument
aw أو or
awqaat أوقات times (multiplying)
awwal أول first
ay naw' أي نوع what kind of?
ay waqt أي وقت what time?
ay أي which?
aydan أيضا also
aydan أيضا likewise
aydan أيضا too (also)
ayluul أيلول September
ayn أين where?
ayyu shakhsin أي شخص anybody, anyone
ibn ابن son
ibna ابنة daughter
ibnat al-'akh ابنة الأخ niece
ibra إبرة needle
ibriiq إبريق jug, pitcher
ibriiq إبريق pitcher, jug
idaafii إضافي further, additional
idaafii إضافي extra
idara ادارة direction
idhaa إذا if
idhin إذن licence, permit
idraak ادراك awareness
ihaana إهانة insult
ihtiraam احترام respect
iimaa' إيماء gesture
iimaan إيمان belief, faith
ijbaarii إجباري compulsory
ikhtibaar اختبار test
ikhtilaaf اختلاف difference (discrepancy in figures)
ikhtilaaf اختلاف difference (in quality)
ikhtiyaari اختياري optional
ila 'ayn الى أين where to?
ila al-jaanib al-'aakhar إلى الجانب الآخر over: to turn over
ila al-khaarij إلى الخارج out
ila al-liqaa' إلى اللقاء goodbye
ila al-liqaa' إلى اللقاء see you later!
ila jaanib إلى جانب next to
ila mata إلى متى how long?

ARABIC–ENGLISH

ila الى to, toward (a place)
ilaah إله god
iliktrunii إلكتروني electronic
illaa ’idhaa الا اذا unless
imra’a امرأة woman
induniisii إندونيسي Indonesian
induniisiya إندونيسيا Indonesia
inkiltra إنكلترا England
inkliizii إنكليزي English
insaan انسان human
intabih انتبه look out!
intaha انتهى over, finished
intikhaabaat انتخابات election
intirniit انترنيت Internet
inzi’aaj انزعاج bother, disturbance
iqtiraah اقتراح suggestion
iqtisaad اقتصاد economy
iqtisaadii اقتصادي economical
irlandaa ايرلندا Ireland
irlandii ايرلندي Irish
i’saar istiwaa’i اعصار استوائي typhoon
isba’ al-qadam اصبع القدم toe
isba’ إصبع finger
isfanj اسفنج sponge
isghaa’ اصغاء listen
ishaara اشارة sign, symbol
islaam إسلام Islam
ism اسم given name
ism اسم name
istiiraad استيراد import
istimaara استمارة form (to fill out)
istinaa’i اصطناعي artificial
ithnaa ’ashar اثنا عشر twelve
ithnayn اثنين two
itraa’ إطراء praise
ittilaa’ إطلاع acquaintance
iz’aaj ازعاج disturbance
udhun أذن ear
ughniya أغنية song
ukht أخت sister
umm أم mother
unthaa أنثى female
unzur أنظر look!
urjuwaanii أرجواني purple
urubba أوروبا Europe
usbuu’iyyan أسبوعيا weekly
usbuu’ أسبوع week
usluub tabikh أسلوب طبخ cuisine, style of cooking
ustraalii استرالي Australian
ustraaliya استراليا Australia
ustuura أسطورة myth
aala haasiba آلة حاسبة calculator
azraq أزرق blue
’aa’ila عائلة family
’aa’iq عائق hindrance
’aa’iq عائق bar (blocking way)
aab آب August
’aada عادة custom, tradition
’aadatan عادة normally
’aadatan عادة usually
’aadii عادي average (so-so, just okay)
’aadii عادي common, frequent
’aadii عادي regular, normal
’aaj عاج ivory
aakhar آخر else: anything else
aakhar آخر else: or else
aala آلة tool, utensil, instrument
’aalamii عالمي international
’aalin عال high
’aam عام general, all-purpose
’aam عام public
’aaqil عاقل reasonable (sensible)
’aaqil عاقل sensible

A

'aar عار shame, disgrace
'aarin عار naked
'aarin عار nude
'aasifa عاصفة storm
'aatifa عاطفة emotion
'aatil 'an al-'amal عاطل عن العمل unemployed
'abra عبر across
'abra عبر via
'abuus عبوس frown
'ada عدا besides
'adad as-sukkaan عدد السكان population
'adad عدد number
'adad عدد figure, number
'adal عضل muscle
addawra ash-shariya الدورة الشهرية period (menstrual)
ad-dii fii dii الدي في دي DVD
adh-dhura as-sukkariyya الذرة السكرية sweetcorn
'adiim al-jadwaa عديم الجدوى useless
'aduw عدو enemy
afdal min من أفضل rather than
'afwan عفوا excuse me! (apology)
'afwan عفوا pardon me? what did you say?
'afwan عفوا sorry!
ahyaanan أحيانا time: from time to time
'ajaban عجبا how strange
ajdaad أجداد grandparents
aj-jaw الجو atmosphere, ambience
ajnabii أجنبي foreign
ajnabii أجنبي foreigner
'ajuuz عجوز old (of persons)
akbara sinnan سنا أكبر elder
akhdar أخضر green
'aksii عكسي backward
'aksii عكسي reversed, backwards
akthar mina l-laazim أكثر من اللازم too (excessive)
akthar أكثر more (comparative)
akthar أكثر more of (things)
al-aan ألان presently, nowadays
al-aan ألان now
al-aan ألان right now
al-arbi'aa' الأربعاء Wednesday
al-aswa' الأسوأ worst
al-ithnayn الاثنين Monday
al-ukht aw al-akh al-akbar الأخت أو الأخ الأكبر older brother or sister
al-usbuu' al-maadii الأسبوع الماضي last week
al-aaliha الآلهة goddess
al-aan ألان just now
al-ahad الأحد Sunday
'ala al-aqal على الأقل least: at least
'ala fikra على فكرة by the way
'alaa al-aqdaam على الأقدام on foot
'alaa t-tariiq على الطريق on the way
'alaa zahr على ظهر on board
'alaa على on, at
al'aab naariyya ألعاب نارية fireworks
al-'aalam العالم world
al-'afw العفو you're welcome!
al-'afw العفو don't mention it!
al-akthar الأكثر most (superlative)
al-akthar الأكثر most (the most of)

ARABIC–ENGLISH

al-'amuud al-fiqrii العمود الفقري spine
'alam علم flag
al-'asaa'ibiyya العصائبية noodles
al-a'shaab al-laymuuniya الأعشاب الليمونية lemongrass
al-ashyaa' al-'atiiqa الأشياء العتيقة antiques
al-baakhira al-'abbaara الباخرة العبارة ferry
al-baanuuraamaa البانوراما panorama
al-baariha البارحة yesterday
al-baariha البارحة last night
al-baazilla البازلا peas
al-baazilla' البازلاء snowpeas
al-babaayaa البابايا papaya
al-bariid البريد post office
al-barkuuli البركولي broccoli
al-biijaama البيجاما nightdress
al-brunz البرونز bronze
al-buuziya البوذية Buddhism
al-diyaana al-masiihiyya الديانة المسيحية Christianity
al-faasuulyia الفاصوليا kidney beans
al-fasuuliya al-khadraa' الفاصوليا الخضراء green beans
al-filippiin الفيليبين Philippines
al-fiyitnaam الفيتنام Vietnam
al-fuulaadh الفولاذ steel
al-haatif al-jawwaal الهاتف الجوال mobile phone
al-habbar الحبار squid
al-hamaa الحماة mother-in-law
al-jamii' الجميع everybody, everyone
al-kaamira الكاميرا video recorder
al-kanna الكنة daughter-in-law
al-karfas الكرفس celery
al-kathiir min الكثير من lots of
al-kathiir الكثير a lot
al-khalf الخلف back, rear
al-khamiis الخميس Thursday
al-khasim الخصم opponent
al-khudaar الخضار greens
al-kiiwii الكيوي kiwi fruit
al-kunfuushiyusiyya الكونفوشيوسية Confucianism
al-kura al-lahmiyya الكرة اللحمية meatball
al-ladhi الذي that, which, the one who
al-ladhii الذي one who, the one which
al-laqab اللقب surname
al-lugha al-fiyitnaamiyya اللغة الفيتنامية Vietnamese
al-ma'khadh المأخذ plug (electric)
almaas ألماس diamond
al-mahaara المحارة oyster
al-makaan al-maqsuud المكان المقصود destination
al-manjaa المنجا mango
al-miftaah al-kahrabaa'ii المفتاح الكهربائي switch
al-muruur المرور traffic
al-muwaalii الموالي next (in line, sequence)
al-muwaalii الموالي following
al-nashshaal النشال pickpocket
al-qaliil القليل a little
al-qirtaasiyya القرطاسية stationery
al-quraydis القريدس prawn
al-qurs al-madghuut القرص المضغوط CD

A

ARABIC–ENGLISH

al-qurs ath-thaabit القرص الثابت hard disk
al-usbuu' al-qaadim الأسبوع القادم next week
al-'uudaan العودان chopsticks
al-wilaayaat al-muttahida al-'amriikiyya الولايات المتحدة الأمريكية United States
al-yaa nasiib اليانصيب lottery
al-yaabaan اليابان Japan
al-yawn اليوم today
a'ma أعمى blind
amaamii أمامي forward
amaana أمانة deposit (leave behind with someone)
'amal عمل job
'amal عمل action
'amal عمل business
amalan أملا hopefully
'amiiq عميق deep
'amm عم uncle
amsi al-awwal امس الأول day before yesterday
amthaal تمثال sculpture
'amuud عمود post, column
amwaaj mutakassira امواج متكسرة surf
'an tariiq عن طريق way: by way of
anaa أنا I, me
'aniid عنيد stubborn, determined
an-naas الناس people
an-najda النجدة help!
'aql عقل mind, brain
aqraas أقراص tablets
'araba عربة cart (pushcart)
'araba عربة cart (horsecart)
'araq عرق sweat
ard أرض Earth, the world
ard أرض ground, earth
ard أرض floor
'ard عرض offering
'ard عرض width
'ard عرض display
'ariid عريض wide
ariika أريكة couch, sofa
'ariis عريس bridegroom
ar-rahim الرحم uterus
ar-rutba الرتبة rank, station in life
'aruus عروس bride
aruz dabiq أرز دبق sticky rice
'asaa عصا stick, pole
'asal عسل honey
'asfuur عصفور bird
'ashaa' عشاء dinner, evening meal
'ashara عشرة ten
'asharaat عشرات tens of, multiples of ten
'asharat 'aalaaf عشرة الاف ten thousand
ash-shahaadaat الشهادات qualification
ash-sharaj الشرج anus
'asiir عصير juice
asla' اصلع bald
asnaan أسنان teeth
asri' أسرع hurry up!
'asrii عصري modern
as-sabaanikh السبانخ spinach
as-sabt السبت Saturday
as-sana al-maadiya السنة الماضية last year
as-sana al-qaadima السنة القادمة next year
as-siin الصين China
as-suuq al-markaziyya السوق المركزية supermarket

a<u>th</u>-<u>th</u>ulaa<u>th</u>aa' الثلاثاء Tuesday
'a<u>t</u>sa عطسة sneeze
'a<u>t</u><u>sh</u>aan عطشان thirsty
a<u>t</u>-<u>t</u>aabiq al-asfal الطابق الأسفل downstairs
at-taa<u>gh</u>aaluu<u>gh</u>iy التاغالوغي Tagalog
a<u>t</u>-<u>t</u>aawiyya الطاوية Taoism
a<u>t</u>-<u>t</u>abii'a الطبيعة a nature
at-tanazzuh التنزه sightseeing
at-tuufuu التوفو tofu
aydan أيضا as well
'ayn عين eye
ayy min من أي either
ayyar أيار May
'ayyina عينة sample
ayyu makaanin أي مكان anywhere
ayyu shay'in أي شيء anything
a'zab أعزب single (not married)
'a<u>z</u>iim عظيم grand, great
'a<u>z</u>iim عظيم great, impressive
'a<u>z</u>m عظم bone
a<u>z</u>-<u>z</u>uhr الظهر afternoon (midday)

B

baa'i' بائع sales assistant
baab باب door
baa<u>dh</u>injaan باذنجان aubergine, eggplant
baa<u>kh</u>ira باخرة ship
baari' بارع skilful
baa<u>t</u>il باطل wrong (morally)
ba'd بعد yet: not yet
ba'<u>d</u> بعض some
ba'da 'i<u>dh</u>in بعد نذ afterwards, then
ba'da a<u>z</u>-<u>z</u>uhr بعد الظهر afternoon (3 pm to dusk)
ba'da l-ghad بعد الغد day after tomorrow

ba'da بعد after
badal بدل instead of
ba<u>dh</u>ra بذرة seed
ba'du بعد already
bahaar بهار pepper, black
ba<u>h</u>ir بحر beach
ba<u>h</u>r بحر sea
ba<u>h</u>th بحث research
ba'iid بعيد far
ba<u>kh</u>uur بخور incense
balaa<u>t</u> بلاط palace (Balinese)
balad بلد country (nation)
balyuun بليون billion
bantaluun بنطلون pants, trousers
banziin بنزين gasoline
banziin بنزين petrol
baqara بقرة cow
baqiyya بقية remainder, leftover
baqiyya بقية rest, remainder
baq<u>sh</u>ii<u>sh</u> بقشش tip (gratuity)
bard برد cold
bariid 'iliktrunii بريد إلكتروني email (system)
bariid jawwy بريد جوي airmail
bariid musajjal بريد مسجل registered post
bariid sa<u>th</u>ii بريد سطحي surface mail
bariid بريد mail, post
barii<u>t</u>aaniya بريطانيا United Kingdom
barnaamaj برنامج show (broadcast)
barnaamaj برنامج broadcast, program, schedule
barq برق lightning
ba<u>s</u>al بصل onion

B

bashara بشرة skin
bashi' بشع ugly
basiit بسيط plain (not fancy)
basiit بسيط simple (easy)
baskawiit بسكويت biscuit (salty, cracker)
baskawiita maaliha بسكويتة مالحة cracker, salty biscuit
baskawiit بسكويتة biscuit (sweet, cookie)
bataataa بطاطا potato
batal بطل champion
batii' بطيء slow
batn بطن abdomen
batta بطة duck
battaaniya بطانية blanket
battiikh بطيخ melon
battiikh بطيخ watermelon
bawwaaba بوابة gate
bayda بيضة egg
baydawii بيضوي oval (shape)
bayna بين among
bayna بين between
baynamaa بينما meanwhile
bayt بيت house
bi'ikhlaas باخلاص truly
bi'r بئر well (for water)
bi-but' ببطء slowly
bidaakhil بداخل inside of
bidaaya بداية start, beginning
bidaaya بداية beginning
biduun بدون without
bii'a بيئة environment, the
biira بيرة beer
bikhusuus بخصوص about (regarding)
bil'ahra بالأحرى rather, fairly
bil'idaafa بالإضافة in addition
bil'idhn بالإذن excuse me! (attracting attention)
bil'idhn بالإذن excuse me! (getting past)
bilad al-ghaal بلاد الغال Wales
bilmi'a بالمئة percent
bil-muqaarana ma'a بالمقارنة مع compared with
bil-muqaarana بالمقارنة opposed, in opposition
bi-lqitaar بالقطار rail: by rail
bilutf بلطف smooth (to go smoothly)
bimaa fii dhalika بما في ذلك included, including
binaa' qadiim بناء قديم temple (ancient)
binafsihi بنفسه own, on one's
bin-nisba 'ilaa بالنسبة إلى concerning, regarding
binnisbati ilaa بالنسبة إلى according to
bint بنت girl
bishiq al-anfus بشق الأنفس barely
bisihhatik بصحتك cheers!
bis-sudfa بالصدفة chance, by
bisur'a بسرعة quickly
bisu'uuba بصعوبة hardly
bitaaqa bariidiyya بطاقة بريدية postcard
biwaasitat بواسطة by means of
biwuduuh بوضوح apparently
blaastiik بلاستيك plastic
briitaani بريطاني British
buhayra بحيرة lake
bukhaar بخار steam
bunni بني brown
buraaz براز shit
burj برج tower
burkaan بركان volcano
burma بورما Burma

burmii بورمي Burmese
burnus hammaam برنس حمام bathrobe
buuza بوظة ice cream
buuzi بوذي Buddhist

D

daa'im دائم permanent
daa'iman دائما always
daa'iman دائما ever, have already
daa'ira دائرة circle
daa'i' ضائع lost (can't find way)
daa'i' ضائع lost property
daa' داء disease
daabit shurta ضابط شرطة police officer
daafi' دافئ warm
daajj ضاج noisy
daakhil داخل inside
dabaab ضباب soup (clear)
dabaab ضباب fog
dabiq دبق sticky
daftar litadwiin al-yawmiyyaat دفتر لتدوين اليوميات diary, daybook
daftar دفتر notebook
daghit ضغط pressure
da'iif ضعيف weak
dajaaj دجاج chicken
dajiij ضجيج noise
dajir ضجر bored
daliil دليل guidebook
daliil دليل proof
dalu دلو bucket
damm دم blood
dammaada ضمادة bandage
daqiiq دقيق exact, exactly
daqiiq دقيق punctual
daqiiqa دقيقة minute
daraj درج steps, stairs
daraja درجة class, category
daraja درجة degree, level
daraja درجة degrees (temperature)
darajaat درجات scales
darar ضرر damage
darba ضربة hit, strike
dariiba ضريبة rate, tariff
darraaja دراجة bicycle
darraja دراجة motorcycle
dars درس lesson
daw' ash-shams ضوء الشمس sunlight
daw' wamdii ضوء ومضي flashlight, torch
daw' ضوء light (lamp)
da'wa دعوة invitation
dawaa' دواء drug (medicine)
dawaa' دواء cure (medical)
dawaajin دواجن poultry
dawla دولة nation, country
dawr دور queue, line
dawr دور role
dayf ash-sharaf ضيف الشرف guest of honour
dayf ضيف guest
dayn دين debt
dayyiq ضيق close together, tight
dayyiq ضيق narrow
dayyiq ضيق tight
dazzina دزينة dozen
dhaalik ذلك that (introducing a quotation)
dhahab ذهب gold
dhakar ذكر male
dhakii ذكي smart
dhakii ذكي clever

F

dhalika, uula'ika ذلك، أولئك that, those
dhaqin ذقن chin
dhayl ذيل tail
dhikrayaat ذكريات memories
dhiraa' ذراع arm
dhubaaba ذبابة fly (insect)
dhubaaba ذبابة mosquito
dhura ذرة corn, grain
didd ضد opposite (contrary)
dif' دفء warmth
dihaan دهان paint
dimaagh دماغ brain
diyaana ديانة religion
diyaanat shintu al-yaabaaniyya ديانة شنتو اليابانية Shinto
duf'a دفعة payment
duhniyyaat دهنيات fat, grease
dukhaan دخان smoke
dulaab دولاب wheel
dumuu' دموع tears
dush دش shower (for washing)
duwali دولي national

F

fa'r فأر mouse (animal)
fa'r فأر rat
fa'ratu l-kambyuutar فأرة الكمبيوتر mouse (computer)
faa'ida فائدة interest (paid by a bank)
faa'ida فائدة interest (paid to a bank)
faa'iz فائز winner
faakhir فاخر fancy
faakiha فاكهة fruit
fa'ala shayan maa فعل شيئا ما have done something
faarigh فارغ empty
faarigh فارغ finished (none left)
faasid فاسد off (gone bad)
faasid فاسد spoiled (of food)
faatir فاتر cool
faatuura فاتورة invoice
faatuura فاتورة receipt
faatuura فاتورة bill
faax فاكس fax (message)
faax فاكس fax (machine)
fahasb فحسب merely
fahis فحص exam, test
faj'atan فجأة suddenly
fajir فجر dawn
fakhidh فخذ thigh
fakhuur فخور proud
fakk فك jaw
famm فم mouth
fann al-'imara فن العمارة architecture
fann فن art
fannaan فنان artist
faqat فقط just, only
faqat فقط only
faqiir فقير poor
faraasha فراشة moth
faraasha فراشة butterfly
fariiq فريق team
fashal فشل failure
fasl فصل season
fatiil فتيل matches
fatuur فطور breakfast, morning meal
fawdaa فوضى mess, in a
fawq فوق above, upstairs
fawqa فوق up, upward
fazz فظ rude
fi al-aghlab في الأغلب mostly
fi alwaaqi' في الواقع actually
fi l-a'laa في الأعلى upstairs

ARABIC–ENGLISH

fidda فضة silver
fii al-waqt al-haadir في الوقت الحاضر present moment, at the
fii haadha l-'asr في هذا العصر nowadays
fii kull makaan في كل مكان everywhere
fii l-maadii في الماضي olden times, in
fii l-masaa' في المساء at night
fii l-waqt al-muhaddad في الوقت المحدد on time
fii في at home
fii في in, at (space)
fii في into
fii في on (of dates)
fiil فيل elephant
fijj فج unripe
fikra فكرة idea
fi'lan فعلا indeed
film li-taswiir al-futtughraafiyy فيلم للتصوير الفوتوغرافي film (camera)
film sinamaa'i فيلم سينمائي film, movie
film فيلم movie
firaash فراش mattress
fitir فطر fungus
fitr فطر mushroom
fitra فترة point (in time)
fitra فترة period (of time)
fulful فلفل chilli, pepper
funduq فندق hotel
funduq فندق lodge, small hotel
furn فرن oven
fursa فرصة chance, opportunity
furshaat asnaan فرشاة أسنان toothbrush
furshaat فرشاة brush
fusuus فصوص cloves
fuul 'aswad فول أسود black beans
fuul suudaanii فول سوداني peanut
fuul فول bean

G

ghaa'ib غائب absent
ghaa'ib غائب missing (absent)
ghaa'im غائم cloudy, overcast
ghaa'im غائم dull (weather)
ghaa'im غائم overcast, cloudy
ghaaba غابة jungle
ghaaba غابة forest
ghaadib غاضب angry
ghaadib غاضب cross, angry
ghaaliban غالبا often
ghaalin غال expensive
ghaamid غامض vague
ghabii غبي stupid
ghadab غضب anger
ghadan غدا tomorrow
ghadhaa' غذاء lunch, midday meal
ghalta غلطة mistake
ghalta غلطة fault
ghanii غني rich
ghanii غني well off, wealthy
gharb غرب west
gharbii غربي westerner
ghariib غريب strange
ghashaawa غشاوة mist
ghashshash غشاش cheat, someone who cheats
ghataa' lir-ra's غطاء للرأس headdress
ghataa' غطاء coat, overcoat
ghayr daruurii غير ضروري unnecessary

ghayr haadd غير حاد mild (not spicy)
ghayr muhadhab غير مهذب impolite
ghayr naadij غير ناضج raw, uncooked, rare
ghayr qaanuuni غير قانوني illegal
ghayr غير other
ghayyuur غيور jealous
ghiira غيرة jealousy
ghilaal al-baashin غلال الباشين passionfruit
ghitaa' al-maa'ida غطاء المائدة tablemat
ghitaa' at-taawila غطاء الطاولة tablecloth
ghitaa' غطاء lid
ghitaa' غطاء sheet (for bed)
ghubaar غبر dust
ghurfa غرفة room (in hotel)
ghurfa غرفة room (in house)
ghurfat an-nawm غرفة النوم bedroom
ghuruub غروب sunset
ghusn غصن branch
ghulf غولف golf

H

haa'it حائط wall
haabit هابط descendant
haad حاد sharp
haadd حاد hot (spicy)
haadhaa حذا this, these
haadhihi al-layla هذه الليلة tonight
haadi' هادئ quiet
haadi' هادئ calm
haadi' هادئ silent
haadir حاضر prepared, ready
haadith حادث accident
haaffa حافة edge
haafila saghiira حافلة صغيرة minibus
haafila / baas حافلة/باص bus
haaja حاجة need
haajib حاجب eyebrow
haakim حاكم leader
haala حالة condition (status)
haala حالة situation, how things are
haalan حالا immediately
haalan حالا at once
haamid حامض lemon, citrus
haamid حامض lime, citrus
haamid حامض sour
haamil حامل pregnant
haarr حار hot (temperature)
haasuub حاسوب computer
haatif naqqaal هاتف نقال cell phone
haatif هاتف telephone
haawil qadra al-mustataa' حاول قدر المستطاع do one's best
habb as-simsim حب السمسم sesame seeds
habl حبل rope
hadaa'iq nabaatiya حدائق نباتية botanic gardens
hadaara حضارة culture
hadaf هدف goal
hadaf هدف purpose
hadath حدث happened, what happened?
hadath حدث happening, incident
hadath حدث event
hadhir حذر cautious
hadiid حديد iron
hadiiqa 'aamma حديقة عامة gardens, park

hadiiqa حديقة garden, yard
hadiiqa حديقة park
hadiiqat al-hayawaanaat حديقة الحيوانات zoo
hadiith حديث conversation
hadiyya هدية present (gift)
hadiyya هدية gift
hafiid حفيد grandchild
hafiid حفيد grandson
hafiida حفيدة granddaughter
hafl حفل party (event)
hafl حفل show (live performance)
hajar حجر stone
hajz حجز reservation
hakiim حكيم wise
halaq حلق ear rings
halawiyaat حلويات confectionery
haliib حليب milk
hallaaq حلاق barber
halq حلق throat
halwa حلوى candy, sweets
halwa حلوى sweet, dessert
hamaasii حماسي exciting
hammaam حمام bathroom
hammaam حمام toilet
hamuu حمو father-in-law
hanaan حنان affection
haqiiba حقيبة suitcase
haqiiba حقيبة briefcase
haqiiqa حقيقة fact
haqil حقل field, empty space
haqqan حقا really (in fact)
haqqan حقا really?
haraamii حرامي thief
haraara حرارة temperature
haraka حركة movement, motion
harb حرب war
harf حرف character (written)
hariir حرير silk
hasad حسد envy
hasan as-suluuk حسن السلوك well-behaved
hasan حسن nice
hasanan حسنا okay
hashara حشرة insect
hasiir حصير mat
hasuud حسود envious
hatta al-'aan حتى الان still, even now
hatta حتى until
hatta حتى even (also)
hattaa حتى so that
hawaa' هواء air
hawla حول round, around
hawla حول around (surrounding)
hayaat حياة life
hayawaan 'aliif حيوان أليف pet animal
hayawaan حيوان animal
haykal هيكل temple (Balinese-Hindu)
hayy حي alive
hayya هيا come on, let's go
haz sayyi' حظ سيء bad luck
haziin حزين sad
haziin حزين upset, unhappy
hazz حظ luck
hazzan sa'iidan حظا سعيدا good luck!
hibr حبر ink
hidhaa' حذاء shoes
hilm حلم dream
himl حمل load
hiraf حرف crafts
hirafii حرفي craftsperson
hirfa حرفة handicraft
hirq حرق burn (injury)

H

hirr هر cat
<u>h</u>isaa' حساء broth, soup
<u>h</u>isaa' حساء soup (spicy stew)
<u>h</u>isaab حساب expense
<u>h</u>i<u>s</u>n حصن fortress
<u>h</u>i<u>ss</u>a حصة portion, serve
hiwaaya هواية hobby
hiya هي she, her
<u>h</u>izaam حزام belt
<u>h</u>izb حزب party (political)
<u>h</u>ubb حب love
<u>h</u>ubuub حبوب pills
<u>h</u>uduud حدود boundary, border
<u>h</u>uduud حدود border (between countries)
<u>h</u>ufra حفرة hole
<u>h</u>ujrat ar-raa<u>h</u>a حجرة الراحة restroom
hujuum هجوم attack (in war)
<u>h</u>ukuuma حكومة government
<u>h</u>ukuuma حكومة officials (government)
<u>h</u>ulw wa <u>h</u>aami<u>d</u> حلو و حامض sweet and sour
<u>h</u>ulw حلو sweet
hum هم they, them
<u>h</u>umma حمى fever
huna هنا present (here)
huna هنا here
hunaak هناك over there
hunaaka هناك there is, there are
hunaaka هناك there
hunkung هونكوهغ Hong Kong
<u>h</u>uqna حقنة injection
<u>h</u>uquul al-'aruzz حقول الأرز rice fields
<u>h</u>uquuq حقوق rights
huraa' هراء nonsense
<u>h</u>urr حر free of restraints
<u>h</u>urriyya حرية freedom
<u>h</u>u<u>s</u>aan حصان horse
huwa هو he, him
<u>h</u>uzayraan حزيران June
<u>h</u>uzn حزن sorrow

I

ibn al-'a<u>kh</u> ابن الأخ nephew
ibn ابن child (offspring)
'iddat عدة several
i<u>h</u>da 'a<u>sh</u>ara احدى عشر eleven
i<u>hd</u>har إحذر careful!
i<u>h</u>tiyaa<u>t</u>iy إحتياطي reserve (for animals)
'iid miilaad sa'iid عيد ميلاد سعيد happy birthday!
'iid miilaad عيد ميلاد birthday
'iid عيد holiday (festival)
ijmaalan إجمال on the whole
'ilm علم science
'inab عنب grapes
'inda عند at
'indamaa عندما when, at the time
'unwaan 'iliktrunii عنوان إلكتروني email address
'iqd عقد necklace
'irq عرق ethnic group
'ishriin عشرين twenty
i<u>st</u>inaa'ii إصطناعي synthetic
'i<u>t</u>r عطر perfume
ittifaaq إتفاق agreement

J

ja'-'a جعة beer
jaa'i' جائع hungry
jaaf جاف dry
jaaf جاف dry (weather)
jaahil جاهل ignorant
jaahiz جاهز done (cooked)
jaahiz جاهز ready

jaami'a جامعة university
jaami' جامع mosque
jaamuus al-maa' جاموس الماء water buffalo
jaar جار neighbour
jabal جبل mountain
jabha جبهة front
jabiin جبين forehead
jadd جد grandfather
jadda جدة grandmother
jadhaab جذاب attractive
jadhdhaab جذاب cute, appealing
jadiid جديد new
jadwal mawaa'iid جدول مواعيد timetable
jafaaf جفاف drought
jamii'an جميعا altogether, in total
jamiil جميل pretty (of women)
jamiil جميل beautiful (of things)
jamiil جميل beautiful (of places)
jamuus جاموس buffalo (water buffalo)
janaah جناح wing
janaaza جنازة funeral
januub gharb جنوب غرب south-west
januub sharq جنوب شرق south-east
januub جنوب south
jariida جريدة newspaper
jasad جسد body
jawaab جواب answer, response (spoken)
jawaab جواب answer, response (written)
jawaab جواب reply, response
jawaarib جوارب socks
jawaaz safar جواز سفر passport
jawz al-hind جوز الهند coconut
jawz جوز pair of, a
jayb جيب pocket
jaysh جيش army
jayyid جيد fine (okay)
jayyid جيد well, good
jazar جزر carrot
jaziira جزيرة island
jiddan جدا mainly
jiddan جدا extremely
jiddii جدي serious (not funny)
jidhir جذر root (of plant)
jiha جهة side
jihaaz ar-rad al'aaliy جهاز الرد الآلي answering machine
jihaaz ar-radd al-'aaliy جهاز الرد الآلي voicemail
jihaaz l-fiidyuu جهاز الفيديو VCR
jihaz lit-tabkh جهاز للطبخ cooker, stove
jild جلد leather
jins جنس sex, gender
jins جنس sex, sexual activity
jinsiyya جنسية nationality
jisir جسر bridge
juzi' جزء bit (part)
jubn جبن cheese
juhd جهد effort
jumla جملة sentence
jumu'a جمعة Friday
jundii جندي soldier
jurh جرح injury, wound
juyuush جيوش troops
juz'iyyan جزئيا partly
juz' جزء part (not whole)
juz' جزء piece, portion, section

K

kaahil كاحل ankle
kaahin كاهن priest
kaamil كامل complete (whole)

K

ARABIC–ENGLISH

K

kaamil كامل finished (complete)
kaamil كامل whole, to be complete
kaanuun al-awwal كانون الأول December
kaaritha كارثة disaster
qaasin قاس cruel
kaatib كاتب writer
kabid كبد liver
kabiir كبير huge
kabiir كبير large, big
kafal كفل bottom (buttocks)
kafal كفل buttocks
kaafin كاف enough
kahif كهف cave
kahrubaa' كهرباء electricity
kahrubaa'ii كهربائي electric
ka'ka, 'ajiin كعكة، عجين cake, pastry
ka'ka muhallaat كعكة محلاة cookie, sweet biscuit
kalb كلب dog
kalima كلمة word
kambuudi كمبودي Cambodian
kambuudia كمبوديا Cambodia
kamm 'umruk كم عمرك how old are you?
kamm كم how many?
kamm كم how much?
kammiyya كمية amount
kaniisa كنيسة church
kanuun ath-thaanii كانون الثاني January
karaahiya كراهية hatred
kariim كريم generous
kartuun كرتون cardboard
kasr كسر break, shatter
kasuul كسول lazy
kathiir at-tawaabil كثير التوابل spicy
kathiir كثير many, much
kathiir كثير so very
kathiir كثير really (very)
kathiiran كثيرا too much
kathiiran كثيرا very, extremely
katif كتف shoulder
kayfa al-haal كيف الحال how are you?
kayfa كيف how?
khaa'if خائف afraid, scared
khaa'if خائف frightened
khaadim خادم servant
khaala / 'amma خالة/عمة aunt
khaarij al-balad خارج البد abroad
khaarij خارج outside
khaarijii خارجي overseas
khaassatan خاصة especially
khaatam خاتم ring (jewellery)
khaathir خاثر thick (of liquids)
khaatib خاطب engaged (to be married)
khabiir خبير expert
khabiith خبيث mean (cruel)
khadd خد cheek
khafiif خفيف light (not heavy)
khafiif خفيف slight
khajlaan خجلان ashamed, embarrassed
khal خل vinegar
khalal خلل defect
khaliij خليج bay
khaliit خليط mixed
khallab خلاب pretty (of places, things)
khamsa خمسة five
khamsata 'ashar خمسة عشر fifteen
khamsiin خمسين fifty
khanziir خنزير pig
khariif خريف autumn

ARABIC–ENGLISH

khariif خريف fall (season)
khariita خريطة map
khaarija خارج outside of
kharuuf خروف lamb, mutton
khasaara خسارة pity: what a pity!
khashab خشب wood
khashabii خشبي wooden
khasib خصب fertile
khasim خصم discount
khasm خصم sale (reduced prices)
khat qutriyy خط قطري diagonally
khata' خطأ error
khata' خطأ false (not true)
khata' خطأ wrong (false)
khatar خطر danger
khatiib خطيب fiancé
khatiiba خطيبة fiancée
khatiir خطير dangerous
khatir خطر serious (severe)
khatiyya خطية fine (punishment)
khatt خط line (mark)
khatt خط lane (of a highway)
khawf خوف fear
khawkh خوخ plum
khayaal az-zill خيال الظل shadow play
khayaal خيال shadow
khayaar خيار choice
khayt خيط thread
khayt خيط string
khidma خدمة service
khilaal خلال while, during
khilaal خلال in (time, years)
khilaal خلال through, past
khitaab خطاب speech
khiyaar خيار cucumber
khizaana خزانة cupboard
khubz خبز bread
khudaar خضار vegetables
khusuusan خصوصا particularly, especially
khusyaat خصيات testicles
khutta خطة plan
khutwa خطوة step
kibriyaa' كبرياء pride
kiilu كيلو kilogram
kilaa كلا both
kilumitir كيلومتر kilometre
kilya كلية kidney
kitaab كتاب book
kuhuul كحول alcohol, liquor
kuhuul كحول spirits, hard liquor
kul كل whole, all of
kulfa كلفة cost (expense)
kull marra كل مرة every time
kull naw' كل نوع every kind of
kull shay' كل شيء everything
kull كل each, every
kull كل all, entire
kullamaa كلما whenever
kullu 'aam wa anta bikhayr كل عام و أنت بخير happy new year!
kura كرة ball
kurat al-madrib كرة المضرب tennis
kurat al-qadam كرة القدم soccer
kurat as-salla كرة السلة basketball
kuriya al-januubiya كوريا الجنوبية Korea, South
kuriya ash-shamaaliya كوريا الشمالية Korea, North
kursii كرسي chair
kursii bilaa zahir كرسي بلا ظهر stool
ariika أريكة armchair
kushk كشك stall (of vendor)
kuub كوب glass (for drinking)

L

kuub كوب cup
kuukh كوخ hut, shack
kuurii كوري Korean
kuusaa كوسا courgettes, zucchini
kuzbara كزبرة cilantro, coriander

L

laa 'ahad لا أحد neither
laa 'ahad لا أحد nobody
laa haadha wa laa dhaalik لا هذا ولا ذلك neither...nor
laa shay' لا شيء nothing
laa taf'al dhaalik لا تفعل ذلك. don't do this
laa... faqat wa laakin لا فقط ولكن not only...but also
laa yahumm لا يهم matter, it doesn't
laa yahumm لا يهم never mind!
laa لا not
laa لا no, not (with verbs)
laa'iha لائحة list
laafita لافتة signboard
laahiqan لاحقا later
laakin لكن however
laakin لكن but
la'alla لعل perhaps, probably
laami' لامع shiny
laawuus لاووس Laos
laawuusii لاووسي Laotian
laaytchii لايتشي lychee
ladhiidh لذيذ tasty
ladhiidh لذيذ delicious
lahaa لها her, hers
lahja لهجة dialect
lahm al-baqar لحم البقر beef
lahm khanziir لحم خنزير pork
lahm mashwii لحم مشوي roast, grill
lahm لحم meat
lahu له his
lahum لهم their, theirs
lahza لحظة moment (in a moment, just a moment)
lahza لحظة moment (instant)
lahza لحظة short time, a moment
lanaa jamii'an لنا جميعا our (excludes the one addressed)
lanaa لنا our (includes the one addressed)
laqab لقب title (of person)
latiif لطيف friendly, outgoing
latiif لطيف pleasant
lawha لوحة painting
lawhat al-mafaatiih لوحة المفاتيح keyboard (of computer)
lawlabii لولبي spiral
lawn لون colour
layl ليل night
layliy ليلي nightly
laymuun ليمون orange, citrus
laymuuni ليموني orange (colour)
laysa ba'du ليس بعد not yet
laysa ليس no, not (with nouns and adjectives)
layyin لين loose (wobbly)
li'ajli لأجل for
li'anna لأن because
li... لـ let's (suggestion)
libaas an-nawm لباس لانوم pyjamas
lidhaa لذا thus, so
lidhaalik لذلك therefore
lidhaalika لذلك so, therefore
lihusn al-haz لحسن الحظ fortunately
lihya لحية beard

ARABIC–ENGLISH

lii لي my, mine
likay لكي in order that, so that
lil'abad للأبد for ever
lil'asaf للأسف regrettably
lil'asaf للأسف unfortunately
lil-bay' للبيع sale, for
limaadha لماذا why?
limaadhaa لماذا what for?
liqaa' لقاء meeting
lisaan لسان tongue
lu'lu' لؤلؤ pearl
lu'ba لعبة game
lu'ba لعبة toy
lu'bat waraq لعبة ورق cards, game
lugha لغة language
lughat bilaad al-ghaal لغة بلاد الغال Welsh

M

ma'a 'anna مع ان although
ma'duba مأدبة banquet
maa 'adaa ما عدا except
ma'a dhaalika مع ذلك though
ma'a مع with
maa' ماء water
maadhaa ماذا what?
maa'iz ماعز goat
maa'iz ماعز sheep
maajungh ماجونغ mah jong
maal مال cash, money
maalih مالح salty
maaliizi ماليزي Malaysian
maaliizyaa ماليزيا Malaysia
maalis مالس smooth (of surfaces)
ma'an معا together
ma'an معا both...and
ma'bad hindiy معبد هندي temple (Indian)
ma'bad siiniy معبد صيني temple (Chinese)
mabdhal مبذل dressing gown
mabnaa مبنى building
ma'dan معدن metal
madanii مدني urban
madfuu' مدفوع paid
madiina مدينة city
madkhal مدخل entrance, a way in
madrasa مدرسة school
mafquud مفقود lost (missing)
mafquud مفقود missing (lost person)
maftuuh مفتوح open
maghli مغلي boiled
maghtas مغطس bath
mahal محل department store
mahall محل shop, store
mahatta محطة stop (bus, train)
mahattat al-banziin محطة البنزين gasoline station
mahattat al-qitaar محطة القطار train station
mahattat banziin محطة بنزين petrol station
mahattat l-baas محطة الباص bus station
mahbil مهبل vagina
mahluul محلول loose (not in packet)
mahrajaan مهرجان festival
mahruuq محروق burned down, out
mahzuuz محظوظ lucky
ma'ida معدة stomach, belly
majaa'a مجاعة famine
majalla مجلة magazine
majjaanii مجاني free of charge
majmuu' مجموع entirety, whole

M

ARABIC–ENGLISH

M

majmuu' مجموع total
majmuu'a مجموعة a group
majnuun مجنون insane
majnuun مجنون crazy
majrooh مجروح hurt (injured)
majruuh مجروح injured
ma'juun 'asnaan معجون أسنان toothpaste
ma'juun samak معجون سمك fish paste
ma'juun معجون jam
makaan maa مكان ما somewhere
makaan مكان place
makhbuuz مخبوز baked
makhfii مخفي hidden
makhraj مخرج exit, way out
maksuur مكسور broken, does not work, spoiled
maksuur مكسور broken, snapped (of bones, etc.)
maksuur مكسور broken off
maksuur مكسور cracked
maktab مكتب office
maktab مكتب desk
maktaba مكتبة library
maktuub biqalam مكتوب بقلم by (author, artist)
malaabis daakhiliyya ملابس داخلية shorts (underpants)
malfuuf siinii ملفوف صيني cabbage, Chinese
malfuuf ملفوف cabbage
malii' مليء full
malik ملك king
malika ملكة queen
ma'luumaat معلومت information
ma'mal معمل factory
mamar ممر lane (alley)
mamnuu' ممنوع forbidden
mamnuun ممنون grateful
mamsha ممشى alley, lane
man من who?
ma'na معنى meaning
manba' منبع source
mansii منسي forgotten
manzil ad-duyuuf منزل الضيوف guesthouse
manzil منزل home, house
maqaal مقال article (in newspaper)
maqaal مقال essay
maq'ad مقعد seat
maqbis socket مقبيس (electric)
maqfuul مقفول locked
maqi' al'antirniit موقع النترنيت website
maqlii مقلي fried
maqluub مقلوب overturned
maqsuud مقصود intended for
maqsuum 'ala مقسوم على divided by
maqtuu' مقطوع closed (road)
ma'quul معقول reasonable (price)
ma'quul معقول possible
maq'uul معقول within reason
maraasim مراسم ceremony
marad مرض illness
ma'raka معركة battle
marfa' مرفئ port
marfa' مرفأ harbour
marhaban مرحبا hello! (on phone)
marhaban مرحبا hello, hi
ma'rifa معرفة knowledge
mariid مريض ill, sick
mariid مريض patient (doctor's)
markab مركب boat

ARABIC–ENGLISH

markaziy مركزي central
marratan مرة once
ma'ruuf معروف popular
mas'uul مسؤول responsible, to be
mas'uul مسؤول authority (person in charge)
mas'uuliyya مسؤولية responsibility
masaa' مساء evening
masaafa مسافة room, space
masaafa مسافة distance
masaafat mashyin مسافة مشي walking distance
masaaha مساحة area
masaariif مصاريف expenses
masbah مسبح swimming pool
mashghuul مشغول busy (doing something)
mashghuul مشغول busy, engaged (telephone)
mashhad مشهد scenery
mashhad مشهد view, panorama
mashhuur مشهور famous
mashrab مشرب bar (serving drinks)
mashwii مشوي roasted, grilled, toasted
masiihii مسيحي Christian
maska مسكة handle
masmuuh an مسموح ان allowed to
masrah مسرح theatre (drama)
masrif مصرف bank (finance)
mataa متى when?
mataar مطار airport
mat'am مطعم restaurant
matar مطر rain
matbakh مطبخ kitchen
matbuukh مطبوخ cooked
mathal مثل example
mathalan مثلا such as, for example
mathalan مثلا example, for
mathuu jayyidan مطهو جيدا well-cooked, well-done
matiin متين firm (mattress)
matjar متجر store, shop
mattaat مطاط rubber
mawaad مواد material, ingredient
mawduu' موضوع topic
maw'idd موعد appointment
mawja موجة wave (in sea)
mawluud مولود born, to be
mawqid موقد stove, cooker
mawqif موقف attitude
mawt موت death
mawz موز banana
mayyit ميت dead
mazhariyya مزهرية vase
mazhar مظهر appearance, looks
mi'a مئة hundred
mi'at alf مئة ألف hundred thousand
midakhkha مضخة pump
miftaah مفتاح key (computer)
mighrafa مغرفة ladle, dipper
mihfaza محفظة purse (for money)
mihfaza محفظة bag
mihfaza محفظة wallet
mihna محنة misfortune
mihna مهنة profession
mihna مهنة work, occupation
mikbah مكبح brake
miknasa مكنسة broom
mil'aqa ملعقة spoon

M

milh ملح salt
milkiyya ملكية property
milyuun مليون million
min jaanib من جانب across from
min fadlik من فضلك please (request for something)
min jadiid من جديد again
min من of, from
min من than
minshafa منشفة towel
mintaqa منطقة region
miqas مقص scissors
miqlaat مقلاة pan
mir'aab مرأب garage (for parking)
mir'aat مرآة mirror
mirfaq مرفق elbow
mirwaha مروحة fan (for cooling)
mis'ad مصعد lift, elevator
mi'sam معصم wrist
misbaah مصباح lamp
mish'al مشعل torch, flashlight
mismaar مسمار nail (spike)
mithil مثل like, as
mithl مثل such
mizalla مظلة umbrella
mu'ahhal مؤهل capable of, to be
mu'ajjal مؤجل postponed, delayed
mu'akhkhara مؤخرة rear, tail
mu'allafaat مؤلفات composition, writings
mu'aqqat مؤقت temporary
mu'assas 'ala مؤسس على based on
mu'aththir مؤثر impressive
mu'lim مؤلم painful
mu'lim مؤلم sore, painful
mu'aadala معادلة equality
mu'aadil معادل equal
mu'aaq معاق handicap
mu'addal معدل average (numbers)
mu'allim معلم teacher
mu'aqqad معقد complicated
mu'aqqam معقم cured, preserved
mubaa'bil-mazaad l-'alani مباع بالمزاد العلني auctioned off
mubaaraat مباراة match, game
mubaasharatan مباشرة straight ahead
mubaa' مباع sold
mubakhkhar مبخر steamed
muballal مبلل wet
mubkir مبكر early
mudallal مدلل spoiled (does not work)
mudawwar مدور round (shape)
mudhakkara مذكرة diary, journal
mud-hik مضحك funny
mudhik مضحك humorous
mudhish مدهش surprising
mudhnib مذنب guilty (of a crime)
mudiif مضيف host
mudiir مدير director (of company)
mudiir مدير manager
mudjir مضجر dull (boring)
mudrik مدرك to be conscious of
mudrik مدرك aware
mufassal مفصل complete (thorough)
mufiid مفيد useful
muftaah مفتاح key (to room)
muftaris مفترس fierce

ARABIC–ENGLISH

mughallaf مغلف envelope
mughlaq مغلق closed (door)
mughlaq مغلق shut
mughram مغرم fond of, to be
muhaadara محاضرة lecture
muhaadir محاضر lecturer (at university)
muhaamii محامي lawyer
muhaawala محاولة attempt
muhabbab محبب lovely
muhaddad محدد definite
muhadhdhab مهذب polite
muhadhdhab مهذب well-mannered
muharrik l-aqraas محرك الأقراص CD-ROM
muharrik محرك motor, engine
muhattam محطم broken, shattered
muhattam محطم destroyed, ruined
muhiit محيط ocean
muhiit محيط surroundings
muhim مهم necessary
muhimm مهم important
muhimm مهم interesting
muhtamm مهتم interested in
mu'jab معجب fan (admirer)
mujawharaat مجوهرات jewellery
mujrim مجرم criminal
mujtahid مجتهد hardworking, industrious
mukayyif alhawaa' مكيف الهواء air conditioning
mukhaddar مخدر numb
mukhaddir مخدر drug (recreational)
mukhattat مخطط striped
mukhattataat مخططات arrangements, planning
mukhayyab مخيب disappointed
mukhbir مخبر reporter
mukhjil مخجل embarrassing
mukhtalif مختلف different, other
mukhtalif مختلف another (different)
mukhtasar مختصر short (concise)
mukhtasar مختصر brief
mukhti' مخطئ wrong (mistaken)
muktafii مكتفي satisfied
mulaa'im ملائم fitting, suitable, compatible
mulaahaza ملاحظة note (written)
mulaahaza ملاحظة notice
mulihh ملح urgent
mumaathil مماثل identical
mumayyaz مميز special
mumayyaz مميز characteristic
mumtaaz ممتاز excellent
mumtalakaat ممتلكات possessions, belongings
mumti' ممتع enjoyable
munaafasa منافسة competition
munaafis منافس rival
munaaqasha مناقشة argument
munaaqasha مناقشة discussion
munaasib مناسب convenient
munammat منمط patterned
munaqqat منقط spotted (pattern)
mun'azil منعزل apart
munazzam منظم orderly, organised
munazzif منظف detergent
mundahish مندهش astonished
mundahish مندهش surprised
mundhu منذ ago

M

mundhu منذ since
munfarid منفرد single (only one)
munfasil منفصل separate
munhadar منحدر slope
munjaz منجز done (finished)
munkhafid منخفض low
munsif منصف just, fair
muntafi' منطفئ off (turned off)
muntahii منتهي gone, finished
muntasaf al-layl منتصف الليل midnight
munza'ij منزعج annoyed
muqadas مقدس sacred
muqaddaman مقدما beforehand, earlier
muqaddas مقدس holy
muqfal مقفل closed (shop)
muqiim مقيم resident, inhabitant
muqrif مقرف disgusting
muraahiq مراهق teenager
murabba'aat مربعات checked (pattern)
murabba' مربع square (shape)
murattab مرتب tidy
murbik مربك confusing
murhaq مرهق weary
murjaan مرجان coral
murr مر bitter
murtaah مرتاح comfortable
murtabik مرتبك confused (in a mess)
murtabik مرتبك puzzled
musaa'ada مساعدة assistance
musaafir مسافر traveller
musaa'id مساعد staff
musaalim مسالم peaceful
musamma مسمى called, named
musattah مسطح flat, smooth
mushaghal مشغل on (turned on)
mushawwash مشوش confused (mentally)
mushkila مشكلة problem
mushkila مشكلة trouble
mushmis مشمس sunny
mushriq مشرق clear (of weather)
musht مشط comb
muslim مسلم Muslim
mustahiil مستحيل impossible
mustaqbal مستقبل future: in future
mustaqiim مستقيم straight (not crooked)
mustaqil مستقل free, independent
mustashfaa مستشفى hospital
mustatiil مستطيل rectangle
mustawaa al-'irtifaa' مستوى الإرتفاع level (height)
mustawaa مستوى level (standard)
mut'a متعة treat (something special)
muta'akhkhir متأخر late
muta'akhkhir متأخر late at night
muta'akhkhir متأخر delayed
mutaabiq مطابق same
mu'taad معتاد usual
mutaah متاح available, to make
muta'awwid متعود used to do something
muta'awwid متعود used to, accustomed
mut'ab متعب worn out, tired
mutabaqqii متبقي left, remaining
mu'tadil معتدل mild (not severe)
mutahammis متحمس excited, eager

ARABIC–ENGLISH

mutajammid متجمد frozen
mutakarrir متكرر frequent
mutallaq مطلق divorced
mutammam متمم complete (finished)
mutanaaghim متناغم harmonious
mutaqaa'id متقاعد retired
mutarjim مترجم interpreter
mutarraz مطرز embroidered
mutashaabih متشابه similar
mutashaabih متشابه alike
mutatallib متطلب fussy, requiring
mutawaadi' متواضع modest, simple (uncomplicated)
mutawaafiq متوافق appropriate
mutawarrit متورط involved
mutawattir متوتر tense
mutayassir متيسر available
mutazawwij متزوج married
muthallaj مثلج chilled
muthallath مثلث triangle
mutii' مطيع obedient
muttafaq 'alayh متفق عليه agreed!
muttali' 'ala مطلع على acquainted, to be
muusiiqaa موسيقى music
muwaajih مواجه opposite (facing)
muwaatin مواطن citizen
muzdahim مزدحم crowded, busy
muzdawij مزدوج double
muz'ij مزعج troublesome, annoying
muzlim مظلم dark
muzlim مظلم dusk

N

naa'im نائم asleep
naadij ناضج ripe
naadil نادل waiter, waitress
naadir نادر rare, scarce
naadiran نادرا rarely, seldom
naafidh نافذ sold out
naafidha نافذة window (in house)
naa'im ناعم gentle
naa'im ناعم soft
na'am نعم yes
naaqis ناقص lacking
naaqis ناقص minus
naar نار fire
nabaat نبات vegetable
nabiidh نبيذ wine
nabta نبتة plant
nabtat al-'aruzz نبتة الأرز rice (plant)
nafsii نفسي self
nahiil نحيل slender
nahiil نحيل slim
nahit نحت carving
nahnu نحن we, us (excludes the one addressed)
nahnu نحن we, us (includes the one addressed)
nahwa نحو to, toward (a person)
najaah نجاح success
najma نجمة star
namir نمر tiger
namuudhaj نموذج pattern, design
namuudhajii نموذجي typical
naqd ma'dani نقد معدني coin
naqii نقي pure
na'saan نعسان sleepy
na'saan نعسان tired (sleepy)
nashaat نشاط activity

Q

na<u>s</u>iiha نصيحة advice
nasiij نسيج weaving
nasiim نسيم wind, breeze
natiija نتيجة result, effect
natiijatan li نتيجة لـ resulting from, as a result
natin نتن rotten
naw' نوع kind, type, sort
naylun نيلون nylon
naysaan نيسان April
nayyi' نيء uncooked
na<u>z</u>aafa نظافة cleanliness
na<u>z</u>iif نظيف clean
na<u>zz</u>aaraat نظارات glasses, spectacles, eyeglasses
nifaaya نفاية garbage
nihaaya نهاية end (finish)
nisba mi'awiyya نسبة مئوية percentage
ni<u>s</u>f نصف half
niyu ziilandaa نيو زلندا New Zealand
nu<u>h</u>aas نحاس copper
nukta نكتة joke
nuq<u>t</u>a نقطة period (end of a sentence)
nuq<u>t</u>a نقطة point, dot
nus<u>kh</u>a نسخة photocopy
nus<u>kh</u>a نسخة copy

Q

qaa'im قائم situated, to be
qaa'imat a<u>t</u>-<u>t</u>a'aam قائمة الطعام menu
qaa'at as-siinimaa قاعة السينما movie house
qaa<u>h</u>il قاحل barren
qaa'ida قاعدة bottom (base)
qaamuus قاموس dictionary
qaanuunii قانوني legal

qaarra قارة continent
qaasin قاس hard (solid)
qaasin قاس rough
qaasin قاس severe
qabiila قبيلة tribe
qabla قبل first, earlier, beforehand
qabla قبل before (in time)
qabr قبر grave
qaddaa<u>h</u>a قداحة lighter
qa<u>dh</u>ir قذر dirty
qa<u>d</u>iib قضيب penis
qadiim قديم old (of things)
qadiim قديم ancient
qadiim قديم worn out (clothes, machine)
qafa<u>s</u> قفص crate
qahwa قهوة coffee
qalam ra<u>s</u>aa<u>s</u> قلم رصاص pencil
qalam قلم pen
qalb قلب heart
qaliil قليل little (not much)
qaliil قليل few
qaliilan قليلا bit (slightly)
qaliilan قليلا slightly
qamar قمر moon
qamiis daa<u>kh</u>ilii قميص داخلي undershirt
qamii<u>s</u> taa'iy قميص تائي teeshirt
qamii<u>s</u> قميص blouse
qamii<u>s</u> قميص shirt
qanniina قنينة bottle
qaraar قرار decision
qariib قريب close to, nearby
qariib قريب around (nearby)
qariiban قريبا soon
qarin قرن century
qarnabii<u>t</u> قرنبيط cauliflower
qarya قرية town
qarya قرية village

R

qaṣab sukkar قصب سكر
sugarcane

qaṣd قصد intention

qaṣiir قصير short (not tall)

qaṣr قصر palace (Javanese)

qawaaniin قوانين laws, rules,
legislation

qawii قوي strong, powerful

qidr قدر pot

qifl قفل lock

qiima قيمة value, good

qimma قمة top

qimma قمة peak, summit

qinaa' قناع mask

qird قرد monkey

qird قرد ape

qirṣ قرص diskette

qirsh قرش shark

qiṣṣa قصة story (tale)

qiṭ'a قطعة item, individual
thing

qiṭ'a قطعة piece, item

qiṭ'a قطعة part (of machine)

qiṭ'a قطعة cut, slice

qiṭaar قطار train

qiyaas قياس size

qiyaas قياس measurement

qubba'a قبعة a hat

qubla قبلة kiss

qumaash قماش cloth

qumaash قماش fabric, textile

quraydis قريدس shrimp, prawn

quṭn قطن cotton

quṭrii قطري diagonal

quwwa قوة power

quwwa قوة strength

quwwa قوة force

R

ra'i رأي opinion

ra'iis al-wuzaraa' رئيس الوزراء
prime minister

ra'iis رئيس president

ra'iis رئيس boss

ra's رأس head

ra'san 'ala 'aqib رأسا على عقب
upside down

ra'smaal رأسمال funds, funding

raa'iḥa kariiha رائحة كريهة
smell, bad odour

raa'i' رائع wonderful

raadiyu راديو radio

raakib راكب passenger

raashid راشد adult

raatib راتب salary

raatib راتب wages

rabb رب God

rabii' saakhin ربيع ساخن hot
spring

rabii' ربيع spring (season)

rabṭat al-'unq ربطة العنق necktie

ra'd رعد thunder

radd رد reaction, response

radda رضة bruise

rafaahii رفاهي luxurious

rafd رفض refusal

rafiiq رفيق friend

raghba رغبة desire

rahiib رهيب terrible

raḥiil رحيل departure

rajul a'maal رجل أعمال
businessperson

rajul رجل man

rakhiiṣ رخيص inexpensive

rakhiiṣ رخيص cheap

ramaadi رمادي grey

raqam l-haatif رقم الهاتف
telephone number

raqiiq رقيق thin (of persons)

raqiiq رقيق bland

S

raqsa رقصة dance
ra<u>sh</u>aa<u>sh</u> رشاش spray
rasim رسم drawing
rasim رسم fee
rasm رسم duty (import tax)
rasmii رسمي official, formal
rassaam رسام drawer
ra<u>t</u>ib رطب humid
ra<u>t</u>ib رطب damp
ri'a رئة lungs
rib<u>h</u> ربح profit
ri<u>h</u>la sa'iida رحلة سعيدة bon voyage!
ri<u>h</u>la رحلة ride (in car)
ri<u>h</u>la رحلة trip, journey
riif ريف country (rural area)
rijl رجل leg
risaala 'iliktruniya رسالة إلكترونية email (message)
risaala رسالة letter
risaala رسالة message
risaala رسالة document, letter
riwaaq رواق corridor
riwaaya رواية novel
riyyaa<u>d</u>a رياضة sports
rubbamaa ربما maybe, perhaps
rubbamaa ربما probably, possibly
rub' ربع quarter
rukba ركبة knee
ru<u>kh</u>sa رخصة permit, licence
ruzma رزمة package

S

saa'i<u>h</u> سائح tourist
saa'il سائل thin (of liquids)
saa'a yadawiyya ساعة يدوية watch (wristwatch)
saa'a ساعة hour
saa'a ساعة clock
saabiq سابق past, former

<u>s</u>aabir صابر patient (calm)
<u>s</u>aabuun صابون soap
<u>s</u>aaha ساحة hall
<u>s</u>aahat ad-dar ساحة الدار courtyard
saahat al-madiina ساحة المدينة square, town square
<u>s</u>aa<u>h</u>ib al-ma<u>h</u>all صاحب المحل shopkeeper
<u>s</u>aa<u>h</u>iba صاحبة girlfriend
saa<u>kh</u>ib صاخب loud
saakin ساكن inhabitant
saam سام poisonous
<u>s</u>aamit صامت still, quiet
<u>s</u>aarim صارم strait
<u>s</u>aarim صارم strict
saa<u>t</u>i' ساطع light (bright)
sa'b صعب hard (difficult)
sab'a سبعة seven
<u>s</u>abaa<u>h</u> صباح morning
<u>s</u>abaa<u>h</u>an صباحا early in the morning
sabab سبب reason, cause
sab'ata 'a<u>sh</u>ar سبعة عشر seventeen
sab'iin سبعين seventy
<u>s</u>abiyy صبي boy
<u>s</u>adiiq صديق boyfriend
<u>s</u>adir صدر chest (breast)
safaara سفارة embassy
safar سفر journey
<u>s</u>aff صف line (queue)
saffuud سفود skewer
<u>s</u>af<u>h</u>a صفحة page
safiir سفير ambassador
<u>s</u>a<u>gh</u>iir صغير little, small, tiny
<u>s</u>a<u>h</u>aafa صحافة press, journalism
<u>s</u>a<u>h</u>aafii صحافي journalist
sa<u>h</u>h صح correct
<u>s</u>a<u>h</u>iih صحيح right, correct

sahiih صحيح true
sahil سهل easy
sahn صحن dish, platter
sahraa' صحراء desert (arid land)
sa'iid سعيد pleased
sa'iid سعيد glad
sa'iid سعيد happy
sajjaada سجادة carpet
sakan سكن accommodation
sakhra صخرة rock
sakraan سكران drunk
salaam سلام greetings
salaat صلاة prayer
salaf سلف ancestor
salb صلب solid
saliim سليم healthy
salla سلة basket
salsa صلصة sauce
salsat al-fulful صلصة الفلفل chilli sauce
salsat as-samak صلصة السمك fish sauce
salsat as-suuyaa (maaliha) صلصة الصويا (مالحة) soy sauce (salty)
salsat as-suuyaa (hulwa) صلصة الصويا (حلوة) soy sauce (sweet)
samaa' سماء sky
samaah سماح forgiveness, mercy
samak سمك fish
samiik سميك thick (of things)
samiin سمين fat, plump
sana سنة year
sana سنة years old
sanawi سنوي annual
sandal صندل sandals
sanghafuura سنغفورة Singapore
saqf سقف ceiling
saqii' صقيع freeze
sarataan سرطان crab
sarii' سريع fast, rapid
sarii' سريع quick
sariih صريح honest
sariir سرير bed
sath سطح surface
sat-hii سطحي shallow
satih سطح roof
sawfa سوف shall, will
sawt صوت voice
sawt صوت sound, noise
saydaliyya صيدلية drugstore, pharmacy
sayf صيف summer
sayniyya صينية tray
sayyaara سيارة vehicle
sayyaara سيارة automobile, car
sayyaarat 'ujraa سيارة أجرة taxi
sayyi' سيء bad
sayyid سيد sir (term of address)
sayyida سيدة lady
sayyida سيدة madam (term of address)
shaab شاب young
shaab شاب youth (young person)
shaafin شاف recovered, cured
shaahid شاهد witness
shaambuu شامبو shampoo
shaarib شارب moustache
shaari' شارع street
shaasha شاشة monitor, screen (of computer)
shaay شاي tea
shabaab شباب youth (state of being young)
shab'aan شبعان full, eaten one's fill
shabah شبح ghost

S

shabaka شبكة net
shabaka شبكة network
shahaada شهادة certificate
shahn شحن truck
shahr شهر month
shajara شجرة tree
shakhs maa شخص ما somebody, someone
shakhs شخص person
shakhsii شخصي own, personal
shakhsii شخصي private
shakhsiya شخصية character (personality)
shakk شك suspicion
shakl شكل form (shape)
shakwa شكوى complaint
shallaal شلال waterfall
sham'a شمع wax
sham'a شمعة candle
shamaal gharb شمال غرب north-west
shamaal sharq شمال شرق north-east
shamaal شمال north
shams شمس sun
shaqqa شقة apartment, flat
shaqqa شقة department
sha'r شعر hair
sharaab شراب drink, refreshment
sharaab شراب soft drink
sharaashif شراشف bedding, bedclothes, bedsheet
shar'ii شرعي valid
shariik شريك partner (in business)
shariit laasiq شريط لاصق tape, adhesive
shariit شريط ribbon
shariit شريط tape recording
shariit شريط cassette
sharika شركة company, firm
sharis شرس wild
sharq شرق east
sharrit tilfizyuunii شريط تلفزيوني TV film
shart شرط condition (pre-condition)
shatranj شطرنج chess
shawka شوكة fork
shay' شيء object, thing
shay' شيء something
shibshib شبشب slippers
shifaah شفاه lips
shirriir شرير naughty
shirriir شرير wicked
shitaa' شتاء winter
shubaat شباط February
shubbaak at-tadhaakir شباك التذاكر counter (for paying, buying tickets)
shubbaak at-tadhaakir شباك التذاكر window (for paying, buying tickets)
shujaa' شجاع brave, daring
shujaa' شجاع stout
shukran شكرا thankyou
shukulaa شوكولا chocolate
shurta شرطة police
shuruuq شروق sunrise
shu'uur شعور feeling
sidriya lil-thadayn صدرية للثديين bra
sifr صفر zero
sihr صهر brother-in-law
sihr صهر son-in-law
siikaar سيكار cigar
siikaara سيكارة cigarette
siinama سينما cinema
siinii صيني Chinese

sijn سجن jail, prison
sikak hadiidiyya سكك حديدية railroad, railway
sikkiin سكين knife
sikritiir سكرتير secretary
sila صلة contact, connection
silaah سلاح weapon
silk سلك wire
sinn سن tooth
si'r at-taasriif سعر التصريف exchange rate
si'r سعر price
si'r سعر rate of exchange (for foreign currency)
sirr سر secret
sirwaal tahtii سروال تحتي panties
sitaara ستارة curtain
sitta ستة six
sittata 'ashar ستة عشر sixteen
sittiin ستين sixty
siwaar سوار bracelet
siyaaj سياج fence
siyaasa سياسة politics
skutlandaa سكوتلندا Scotland
skutlandii سكوتلندي Scottish, Scots
su'aal سؤال question
su'aal سعال cough
sudda سدة plug (bath)
sudfatan صدفة accidentally, by chance
sudra صدرة vest, undershirt
sufuuf صفوف classes (at university)
sukkar سكر sugar
sulahfaat l-bahr سلحفاة البحر turtle (sea)
sulahfaat سلحفاة turtle (land)
sulb صلب stiff
sullam mutaharrik سلم متحرك escalator
sullam سلم ladder
sulta سلطة authority (power)
summ سم poison
sunduuq ma'luumaat صندوق معلومات information booth
sunduuq صندوق box, chest
sur'a سرعة speed
sutra سترة coat, jacket
suu' tafaahum سوء تفاهم misunderstanding
suuf صوف wool
suuq سوق market
suura صورة photograph, picture

T

ta'diya تأدية performance
ta'khiir تأخير delay
ta'miin تأمين guarantee
ta'miin تأمين insurance
ta'shiira تأشيرة visa
ta'thiir تأثير influence
taa'ira طائرة airplane, plane
ta'aam طعام food
taabaq طابق storey (of a building)
taabi' طابع stamp (postage)
taalib طالب schoolchild
taaqa طاقة energy
taariikh al-miilaad تاريخ الميلاد date of birth
taariikh تاريخ history
taariikh تاريخ date (of the month)
taawila طاولة table
taazaj طازج fresh
tabaadul تبادل exchange, to (money, opinions)

T

ARABIC–ENGLISH

T

tab'an طبعا certainly!
tab'an طبعا of course
tabaq طبق plate
tabaq طبق bowl
tabaq طبق dish (particular food)
tabaqa طبقة layer
tabbaakh طباخ cook (person)
tabiib طبيب doctor
tabii'ii طبيعي normal, natural
tabkh طبخ cooking, cuisine
tadarruj تدرج sequence, order
tad-hiya تضحية sacrifice
tadhkaar تذكار souvenir
tadhkirat al-'awda تذكرة العودة return ticket
tadhkirat ittijaah waahid تذكرة إتجا واحد one-way ticket
tadhkira تذكرة ticket (for entertainment)
tadriib تدريب practice
tadriijiyyan تدريجيا gradually
tafaddal تفضل please (go ahead)
taghyiir basiit تغيير بسيط change, small
tahaaniina تهانينا congratulations!
tahaddi تحدي challenge
tahajjum تهجم attack (with words)
tahiin طحين flour
tahta تحت below, downstairs
tahta تحت down, downward
tahta تحت under
ta'iis al-haz تعيس الحظ unlucky
tajriba تجربة experience
takhfiif تخفيف reduction
talab طلب order (placed for food, goods)
talid تلد birth, to give
talla تلة hill
ta'm طعم taste
tamaam as-saa'a تمام الساعة o'clock
tamaaman تماما exactly! just so!
tamaaman تماما completely
tamaatim طماطم tomato
tamanniyaat bi-shifaa' al-'aajil تمنيات بالشفاء العاجل get well soon!
tamdiid تمديد extension (telephone)
tammuuz تموز July
tamriin تمرين training
tanbiih تنبيه warning
tannuura تنورة skirt
taqaatu' تقاطع intersection
taqim طقم set
taqliidii تقليدي traditional
taqm طقم suit, business
taqriiban تقريبا almost, nearly
taqriiban تقريبا around (approximately)
taqriiban تقريبا about, roughly, approximately
taqriiban تقريبا more or less
taqriir تقرير report
taqs طقس climate
taqs طقس weather
taraf طرف tip (end)
taraf طرف border, edge
tard طرد parcel
tariiq طريق road
tariiqa طريقة way, method
tarkhiis ترخيص licence (for driving)
tartiib ترتيب order, sequence
tartiib ترتيب ranking
tasaadum تصادم collision
tasbiqa تسبقة advance money, deposit

ARABIC–ENGLISH

tasdiir تصدير export
tasliya تسلية pastime
tasriif تصريف change, exchange (money)
tatawwur تطور development
tathaa'ub تثاؤب yawn
tat'iim تطعيم vaccination
tatriiz تطريز embroideryb
tawaabil توابل spices
tawaari' طوارئ emergency
tawaqqaf توقف stop it!
tawiil طويل long (time)
tawiil طويل tall
tawqii' توقيع signature
tayaraan طيران flight
taylandaa تايلندا Thailand
taylandii تايلندي Thai
tayyib طيب kind, good (of persons)
thaabit ثابت firm (definite)
thaalith ثالث third
thaanawii ثانوي minor (not important)
thaaniya ثانية second
thadyi ثدي breasts
thalaatha ثلاثة three
thalaathata 'ashar ثلاثة عشر thirteen
thalaathiin ثلاثين thirty
thalj ثلج ice, snow
thallaaja ثلاجة refrigerator
thamaaniin ثمانين eighty
thamaaniya ثمانية eight
thamaaniyata 'ashara ثمانية عشر eighteen
thaman ثمن cost (price)
thaqaafa ثقافة education/culture
thaqiil ثقيل heavy
thawb as-sibaaha ثوب السباحة swimming costume, swimsuit
thawb ثوب garment
thawb ثوب dress, frock
thiqa ثقة confidence
thiyaab an-nawm ثياب النوم nightclothes, pajamas
thiyaab daakhiliyya ثياب داخلية underpants, underwear
thiyaab ثياب clothes, clothing
thumma ثم then
thuqb al-anf ثقب الأنف nostril
dhuu qiima ذو قيمة worth, to be
thuum ثوم garlic
tibb طب medicine
tibbii طبي medical
tifl طفل kid
tifl child (young person)
tijaara تجارة trade, business
tilfaaz تلفاز television, TV
tilmiidh تلميذ pupil, student
timthaal تمثال statue
tis'ata 'ashar تسعة عشر nineteen
tis'a تسعة nine
tis'iin تسعين ninety
tishriin al-'awwal تشرين الأول October
tishriin ath-thaani تشرين الثاني November
tubbaan تبان shorts (short trousers)
tuffaaha تفاحة apple
tuhiid تحيض menstruate, to
tumtir تمطر rain, to
turaab تراب earth, soil
turaab تراب sand
tuthlij تثلج snow, to
tuufaan طوفان flood
tuul طول long (length)

U

'udwu عضو member
'ulba ma'daniya علبة معدنية can, tin
'ulba علبة box (cardboard)
'umla عملة currency
'umr عمر age
'umr عمر lifetime
'umuuman عموما generally
'unuq عنق neck
'unwaan عنوان address
'unwaan عنوان title (of book, film)
'ushb عشب grass
'ushsh عش nest
ustuura أسطورة legend
'utla عطلة day off
'utla عطلة holiday (vacation)
'utlat nihaayat al-usbuu' عطلة نهاية الأسبوع weekend

W

wa و and
wa laa makaan ولا مكان nowhere
wa laa و لا nor
wa ma'a dhaalika و مع ذلك Nevertheless
waabil mina l-matar وابل من المطر shower (of rain)
waadii وادي valley
waahid واحد one
waajib واجب duty (responsibility)
waaqi' واقع located, to be
waasi' واسع broad, spacious
wadii'a وديعة deposit (put money in the bank)
wahiid وحيد sole, only
wahiid وحيد alone
wahiid وحيد lonely
wajba وجبة meal
wajih وجه face
waq'a وقعة fall
waqt وقت time
waraa' وراء behind
waraa' وراء beside
waraq as-sajaa'ir ورق السجائر clove cigarette
waraq ورق paper
waraqa naqdiyya ورقة نقدية note (currency)
waraqa ورقة sheet (of paper)
waraqat nabaat ورقة نبات leaf
warshat tasliih ورشة تصليح garage (for repairs)
wasat al-madiina وسط المدينة downtown
wasat وسط centre (of city)
wasat وسط centre, middle
wasat وسط middle: be in the middle of doing
wasfa tibbiyya وصفة طبية prescription
wasfa وصفة recipe
wasiim وسيم beautiful (of people)
wasiim وسيم handsome
watar وتر tendon
wazn وزن weight
wazza وزة Goose
wisaada وسادة pillow
wusuul وصول arrival

Y

ya'khudh يأخذ take, to remove
ya'kul يأكل eat, to
ya'mur يأمر command, to
ya'mur يأمر order, to command
ya'tii يأتي come, to
yaa ilahii يا إلهي goodness!

yaa la-l'asaf يا للأسف shame: what a shame!
yaabaani ياباني Japanese
yabda' يبدأ begin, to
yabda' يبدأ originate, come from
yabda' يبدأ start, to
yabduu يبدو seem, to
yabhath يبحث search for, to
yabhath يبحث look up (find in book)
yabhath يبحث research, to
yabhath يبحث seek, to
yabii' يبيع sell, to
yabii' bil-mazaad l-'alani يبيع بالمزاد العلني auction, to
yabiit يبيت stay overnight, to
yabkii يبكي cry, to
yabkii يبكي weep, to
yablugh يبلغ attain, reach
yabni يبني build, to
yabqaa يبقى stay, remain
yabrud يبرد cool, to
yabruz يبرز stick out, to
yabtali' يبتلع swallow, to
yabtasim يبتسم smile, to
ya'bud يعبد worship, to
ya'bur يعبر pass, go past
ya'bur يعبر cross, go over
yada' يضع place, put
yada' يضع slip (petticoat, underskirt)
yad'am يدعم back up, to
yadd يد hand
yadda'ii يدعي pretend, to
yadfa' يدفع push, to
yadfa' يدفع pay, to
yadghat يضغط press, to
yadhak 'ala يضحك على laugh at, to
yadhak يضحك laugh, to
yadhan يدهن paint, to (house, furniture)
yadhhab يذهب go, to
yadhkur يذكر mention, to
yadiin يدين owe, to
yadkhul يدخل enter, to
yadkhul يدخل come in
yadnu يدنو approach, to (in time)
yad'uf يضعف weight, to lose
yadull يدل point out
yadumm يضم join, go along
yaduqq يدق knock, to
yad'uu يدعو invite, to (ask along)
yad'uu يدعو invite, to (formally)
yaduur يدور turn around, to
yaf'al يفعل act, to
yaf'al يفعل make do
yaf'al يفعل do, perform an action
yafham يفهم understand, to
yafhas يفحص examine, to
yafhas يفحص inspect, to
yafhas يفحص check, verify
yafruk يفرك scrub, to
yafshal يفشل fail, to
yafsil يفصل separate, to
yaftah يفتح open, to
yaftarid يفترض suppose, to
yaghish يغش cheat, to
yaghlib يغلب beat (to defeat)
yaghlii يغلي boil, to
yaghraq يغرق drown, to
yaghsil as-suhuun يغسل الصحون wash the dishes
yaghsil يغسل wash, to
yaghtasil يغتسل shower, to take a

Y

ARABIC–ENGLISH

Y

yahbit يهبط land, to (plane)
yahdur يحضر attend to
yahduth يحدث happen, occur
yahfaz sirr يحفظ سر secret, to keep a
yahfaz يحفظ keep, to
yahfaz يحفظ leave behind for safekeeping
yahfaz يحفظ save, keep
yahill يحل resolve, to (a problem)
yahill يحل solve, to (a problem)
yahill يحل sort out, deal with
yahjiz يحجز reserve, to (ask for in advance)
yahkum يحكم lead (to be a leader)
yahliq يحلق shave, to
yahlum يحلم dream, to
yahmi يحمي defend (in war)
yahmil يحمل pick up, lift (something)
yahmil يحمل carry, to
yahqun يحقن inject, to
yahrab يهرب run away
yahriq يحرق burn, to
yahrus يحرس guard, to
yahrus يحرس watch over, guard
yahsub يحسب calculate
yahsud يحصد sweep, to
yahtaaj يحتاج need, to
yahtafil يحتفل celebrate, to
yahtajj يحتج protest, to
yahtam bi يهتم بـ look after
yahtam bi يهتم بـ care for, to take
yahtarim يحترم respect, to
yahtariq يحترق on fire
yahuzz يهز swing, to
yahzim يحزم pack, to
yahzim يهزم defeat, to
ya'id يعد promise, to
ya'iish يعيش live (be alive)
yajhaz يجهز ready, to get
yajib يجب have to, must
yajib يجب ought to
yajid يجد find, to
yajiff يجف dry out (in the sun)
yajlib يجلب bring, to
yajlis يجلس sit down, to
yajlis يجلس sit, to
yajma' يجمع assemble, gather
yajni يجني earn, to
yajrah يجرح hurt, to (cause pain)
yakbah يكبح restrain, to
yakbah يكبح brake, to
yakbur يكبر grow larger, to
yakbur يكبر grow up (child)
yakdhib يكذب lie, tell a falsehood
yakfii يكفي satisfy, to
yakhbiz يخبز bake, to
yakhda' يخدع deceive, to
yakhda' يخضع undergo, to
yakhdim يخدم serve, to
yakhla' يخلع take off (clothes)
yakhliq يخلق create, to
yakhlut يخلط mix, to
yakhruj يخرج go out, exit
yakhsir يخسر lose money, to
yakhsir يخسر lose, be defeated
yakhtaar يختار pick, choose
yakhtaar يختار select, to
yakhtaar يختار choose, to
yakhtabir يختبر test, to
yakhtari' يخترع invent, to
yakhtari' يخترع make up, invent
yakhtim يختم stamp (ink)

yakhzin يخزن store, to
ya'kis يعكس reflect, to
yakrah يكره hate, to
yakrah يكره dislike, to
yak<u>sh</u>if يكشف reveal, to (make visible)
yaksir يكسر break apart, to
yakta<u>sh</u>if يكتشف discover, to
yaktub يكتب compose, write (letters, books, music)
yaktub يكتب note down, to
yaktub يكتب write, to
yakuun يكون exist, to
-**yakuun** يكون be, exist
yakwii يكوي iron, to (clothing)
yal'ab يلعب play, to
yalbas يلبس dressed, to get
yalfaz يلفظ pronounce, to
yul<u>gh</u>i يلغي cancel
yul<u>gh</u>i يلغي hold back
yal<u>h</u>aq يلحق follow along, to
yal<u>h</u>as يلحس lick, to
yalmas يلمس touch, to
yaltaqii يلتقي meet, to
yaluum يلوم blame, to
ya'mal يعمل function, to work
yamda<u>gh</u> يمضغ chew, to
yamiin يمين right-hand side
yamla' al-faraa<u>gh</u> يملأ الفراغ fill out (form)
yamla' يملأ fill, to
yamlik يملك own, to
yamlik يملك possess, to
yamna' يمنع hinder, to
yamna' يمنع forbid, to
yamrad يمرض sick to be (vomit)
yamsa<u>h</u> يمسح wipe, to
yam<u>sh</u>ii يمشي walk, to
yamudd at-<u>t</u>aawila يمد الطاولة lay the table

yamurr يمر past: go past
yamu<u>ss</u> يمص suck, to
yamuut يموت die, to
yamzuj يمزج shake something, to
yanaal ينال get, receive
yanaam ينام go to bed
yanaam ينام sleep, to
yan'a<u>t</u>if ينعطف turn, make a turn
yanbut ينبت grow, be growing (plant)
yandam يندم regret, to
yanhad ينهض get up (from bed)
yan<u>h</u>at ينحت sculpt, to
yan<u>h</u>at ينحت carve, to
ya'nii يعني mean, to (word)
yanja<u>h</u> ينجح manage, succeed
yanja<u>h</u> ينجح pass, to (exam)
yanja<u>h</u> ينجح succeed, to
yanjuu ينجو survive, to
yan<u>kh</u>afid ينخفض decline (get less)
yanqul ينقل lift (ride in car)
yanqu<u>s</u> ينقص decrease, to
yanqu<u>sh</u> ينقش engrave, to
yansa ينسى forget about, to
yansa ينسى forget, to
yansa ينسى leave behind by accident
yansa<u>h</u> ينصح advise, to
yansa<u>kh</u> ينسخ photocopy, to
yan<u>sh</u>a' ينشأ develop, to (happen)
yan<u>sh</u>ul ينشل pickpocket, to
yan<u>sh</u>ur ينشر publish, to
yansij ينسج weave, to
yantabih ينتبه pay attention
yantahi ينتهي end, to
yanta<u>kh</u>ib ينتخب vote, to

ARABIC-ENGLISH

Y

yantami ينتمي belong to
yantazir ينتظر wait for, to
yanzur ينظر look at, see
yaqa' يقع fall over
yaqbad يقبض collect payment, to
yaqbal يقبل accept, to
yaqbid 'ala يقبض على capture, to
yaqdii 'alaa يقضى على finish off, to
yaqdir 'alaa يقدر على afford, to
yaqfil يقفل lock, to
yaqfiz يقفز jump, to
yaqif bid-dawr يقف بالدور queue, to line up
yaqif bis-saff يقف بالصف line up, to
yaqif يقف stand up, to
yaqif يقف stand, to
yaqiis يقيس try on (clothes)
yaqiis يقيس measure, to
yaqiz يقظ awake
yaqlaq يقلق worry, to
yaqlii يقلي fry, to
yaqra' يقرأ read, to
yaqsid يقصد intend, to
yaqsid يقصد mean, to (intend)
yaqtarib يقترب approach, to (in space)
yaqtarih يقترح offer, suggest
yaqtarih يقترح recommend, to
yaqtarih يقترح suggest, to
yaqtul يقتل kill, murder
yaquss يقص tell, to (a story)
yaquud يقود lead (to guide someone somewhere)
yaquul يقول say, to
yaquum bijuhd يقوم بجهد effort, to make an
yar'a يرعى take care of, to
yaraa يرى see, to
ya'raq يعرق perspire, to
ya'raq يعرق sweat, to
yarbah يربح win, to
yarbit يربط tie, to
yarfa' يرفع lift, raise
yarfa' يرفع raise, lift
yarfud يرفض refuse, to
yarfud يرفض decline (refuse)
yarghab يرغب desire, to
yarhal يرحل depart, to
ya'rif يعرف know, be acquainted with
ya'rif يعرف know, to
yarinn يرن ring, to (bell)
yarji' يرجع come back
yarji' يرجع back, to go
yarji' يرجع return, go back
yarji' يرجع reverse, to back up
yarkab يركب board, to (bus, train)
yarkab يركب get on (transport)
yarkab يركب ride, to (animal)
yarkab يركب ride, to (transport)
yarkud يركض run, to
yarmii يرمي throw, to
yarqus يرقص dance, to
yarsum يرسم draw, to
yarsum يرسم paint, to (a painting)
yartaah يرتاح relax, to
yartaah يرتاح rest, to relax
yartabit يرتبط connect together, to
yartadii يرتدي put on (clothes)
yartadii يرتدي wear, to
yartafi' يرتفع rise, increase
yartajif يرتجف shiver, to
yartajj يرتج shake, to
ya'rid يعرض display, to

ARABIC–ENGLISH

yarudd 'ala l-haatif يرد على الهاتف answer the phone
yarudd يرد reply, to (in speech)
yarudd يرد reply, to (in writing or deeds)
yarudd يرد respond, react
yas'al يسأل enquire, to
yas'al يسأل ask about, to
yasaar يسار left-hand side
yas'ad يصعد rise, ascend
yas'ad يصعد climb onto, into
yasbah يسبح swim, to
yasbah يسبح bathe, swim
yashab يسحب pull, to
yashaq يسحق beat (to strike)
yashhad يشهد witness, to
yashkur يشكر say thankyou
yashkur يشكر thank, to
yashrab يشرب drink, to
yashrah يشرح explain, to
yashtaaq يشتاق miss, to (loved one)
yashtari يشتري buy, to
yashukk يشك suspect, to
yashukk يشك doubt, to
yashumm يشم smell, to
yash'ur bidh-dhanb يشعر بالذنب guilty, to feel
yash'ur يشعر feel, to
yashwii يشوي grill, to
yasif يصف describe, to
yasil يصل join together, to
yasil يصل reach, get to
yasil يصل arrive, to
yaskun يسكن live (stay in a place)
yasma' يسمع hear, to
yasmah يسمح allow, permit
yasmah يسمح let, allow
yasmin يسمن weight, to gain
yasma' يسمع listen to
yasna' يصنع make, to
yasna' يصنع manufacture, to
yasna' يصنع produce, to
yasqut يسقط fall, to
yasrif يصرف spend, to
yasriq يسرق steal, to
yasrukh يصرخ cry out, to
yasrukh يصرخ yell, to
yasrukh يصرخ shout, to
yasta'jir يستأجر rent out, to
yastaad يصطاد fish, to
yastad'ii يستدعي call, summon
yastaghriq fi ahlaam al-yaqaza يستغرق في أحلام اليقظة day-dream, to
yastahim يستحم bathe, take a bath
yasta'iir يستعير borrow, to
yastalim يستلم receive, to
yastalqii يستلقي lie down, to
yasta'mil يستعمل use, to
yastamti' يستمتع enjoy oneself, to
yastamti' يستمتع enjoy, to
yastashiir يستشير consult, talk over with
yastatii' يستطيع can, be able to
yastatii' يستطيع could, might
yastatii' يستطيع may
yastayqiz يستيقظ awake, wake up
yasubb يصب pour, to
yas'ul يسعل cough, to
yasuum يصوم fast, to
yasuuq يسوق drive, to (a car)
yata'ammal يتأمل hope, to
yata'aawan يتعاون go along, join in, help with
yata'adhdhab يتعذب suffer, to

yata'allam يتعلم learn, to
yata'allam يتعلم study, learn
yata'arra يتعرى undressed, to get
yata'arraf يتعرف recognise, to
yata'a<u>tt</u>al يتعطل break down, to (car, machine)
yata'a<u>tt</u>al يتعطل stuck, won't move
yatabaadal يتبادل trade, to exchange
yatabawwal يتبول urinate, to
yatadarrab يتدرب practice, to
yata<u>dh</u>akkar يتذكر remember, to
yata<u>dh</u>ammar يتذمر complain, to
yata<u>dh</u>awwaq يتذوق taste, to (salty, spicy)
ya'ta<u>dh</u>ir يعتذر apologise, to
ya'ta<u>dh</u>ir يعتذر say sorry
yatafaa'al يتفاعل react to
yata<u>gh</u>allab 'alaa يتغلب على overcome, to
yata<u>h</u>aa<u>sh</u>a يتحاشى ignore, to
yata<u>h</u>aa<u>sh</u>a يتحاشى prevent, to
yatahajjaa يتهجى spell, to
yata<u>h</u>arrak يتحرك move, to
yata<u>h</u>assan يتحسن better, get (improve)
yatakallam 'an يتكلم عن talk about
yatakallam يتكلم speak, to
yatakallam يتكلم talk, to
yata<u>kh</u>aasam min ajli يتخاصم من اجل fight over, to
yata<u>kh</u>alla<u>s</u> min يتخلص من rid: get rid of
yata<u>kh</u>ayyal يتخيل imagine, to
yatalaa'ab يتلاعب play around
yatamanna يتمنى wish, to
yatama<u>sh</u><u>sh</u>a يتمشى go for a walk
ya'tamid 'ala يعتمد على depend on, to
yatanaafas يتنافس compete, to
yatanaawal al-'a<u>sh</u>aa' يتناول العشاء dinner, to eat
yatanaawal al-fatuur يتناول الفطور breakfast, to eat
yatanaawal al-<u>gh</u>a<u>dh</u>aa' يتناول الغذاء lunch, to eat
yatanaqqal يتنقل move from one place to another
yataqaddam' يتقدم advance, go forward
yataqayya' يتقيأ vomit, to
ya'taqid يعتقد consider (to have an opinion)
yataraasal يتراسل correspond (write letters)
yatarajjal يترجل get off (transport)
ya'tari<u>d</u> يعترض object, to protest
ya'tarif يعترف admit, confess
yata<u>s</u>aadam يتصادم collide, to
yatasalla يتسلى fun, to have
yatasallaq يتسلق climb up (hills, mountains)
yatasallaq يتسلق go up, climb
yatasarrab يتسرب leak, to
yata<u>s</u>arraf يتصرف behave
yatasawwaq يتسوق shop, go shopping
yata<u>sh</u>aajar يتشاجر fight, to (physically)
yatawajja' يتوجع ache, to
yatawajjah يتوجه head for, toward

yatawaqqa' يتوقع expect, to
yatawaqqaf يتوقف stop, to cease
yatazawwaj يتزوج marry, get married
yatba' يتبع follow behind, to
yatba' يطبع print, to
yatba' يطبع type, to
yatbukh يطبخ cook, to
yatfa' يطفأ go out (fire, candle)
yathiq يثق confidence, to have
yathiq يثق trust, to
yathqub يثقب pierce, penetrate
yatiir يطير fly, to
ya'tis يعطس sneeze, to
yatlub يطلب ask for, request
yatlub يطلب request, to (formally)
yatlub يطلب request, to (informally)
yatlub يطلب demand, to
yatlub يطلب order something, to
yatrud يطرد chase away, chase out
yatrud يطرد fire someone, to
yatruk يترك leave behind on purpose
yatruk يترك leave, depart
yatruk يترك desert, to abandon
yattahim يتهم accuse, to
yattasil يتصل call on the telephone
yattasil يتصل contact, get in touch with
yattasil يتصل ring, to (on the telephone)
yattasil يتصل dial, to (telephone)
yatwi يطوي fold, to
ya'udd يعض bite, to
ya'uud يعود go home
ya'uud يعود return home, to
ya'uud يعود go back
yawm يوم day
yawm يوم day of the week
yawmiyyan يوميا daily
yazhar يظهر appear, become visible
yazhar يظهر look, seem, appear
yaziid يزيد increase, to
yazin يزن weigh out, to
yazin يزن weigh, to
yazra' يزرع grow, cultivate
yazra' يزرع plant, to
yazun يظن think, to have an opinion
yazuur يزور go around, visit
yazuur يزور stop by, to pay a visit
yu'ajjil يؤجل postpone, to
yu'ajjil يؤجل put off, delay
yu'ajjir يؤجر hire, to
yu'ajjir يؤجر rent, to
yu'ammin يؤمن guarantee, to
yu'assis يؤسس establish, set up
yu'athir fi يؤثر في affect, to
yu'aththir يؤثر influence, to
yu'aththir يؤثر impression, to make an
yu'min يؤمن believe, to
yu'aalij يعالج treat, to (medically)
yu'aamil يعامل treat, to (behave towards)
yu'aaniq يعانق embrace, to
yu'aarid يعارض mind, to be displeased
yu'aarid يعارض oppose, to
yu'allim يعلم teach, to

Y

ARABIC–ENGLISH

Y

yu'alliq يعلق hang, to
yu'arrif يعرف introduce oneself, to
yu'arrif يعرف introduce someone, to
yubaddil يبدل switch, to change
yuballil يبلل soak, to
yub<u>h</u>ir يبحر sail, to
yub'id يبعد throw away, throw out
yudaafi' يدافع defend (with words)
yudaafi' يدافع plead, to
yu<u>d</u>a<u>hh</u>i يضحي sacrifice, to
yuda<u>khkh</u>in يدخن smoke, to (tobacco)
yudallik يدلك massage, to
yudayyi' يضيع lose, mislay
yu<u>dh</u>akkir يذكر remind, to
yu<u>d</u>iif يضيف add, to
yudirr يضر damage, to
yudrik يدرك realise, be aware of
yufa<u>dd</u>il يفضل prefer, to
yufakkir يفكر think, to ponder
yufakkir يفكر consider (to think over)
yufattish يفتش look for
yufawwit يفوت miss, to (bus, flight)
yu<u>gh</u>allif يغلف wrap, to
yu<u>gh</u>anni يغني sing, to
yu<u>gh</u>a<u>tt</u>i يغطي close, to cover
yu<u>gh</u>a<u>tt</u>i يغطي cover, to
yu<u>gh</u>ayyir ra'yahu يغير رأيه change one's mind
yu<u>gh</u>ayyir يغير replace, to
yu<u>gh</u>ayyir يغير change, switch (clothes)
yu<u>gh</u>ayyir يغير change, to (conditions, situations)
yu<u>gh</u>liq يغلق shut, to
yu<u>h</u>aarib يحارب war, to make
yu<u>h</u>aawil to يحاول attempt
yuhaddid يهدد threaten, to
yu<u>h</u>addid يحدد fix, to (a time, appointment)
yu<u>h</u>a<u>dd</u>ir يحضر prepare, make ready
yu<u>h</u>ammil يحمل load up, to
yu<u>h</u>aqqiq يحقق fulfil
yuharrib يهرب smuggle, to
yu<u>h</u>a<u>tt</u>im يحطم destroy, to
yu<u>h</u>awwil 'ila naqid يحول إلى نقد cash a check, to
yu<u>hd</u>ir يحضر fetch, to
yu<u>h</u>ib يحب like, be pleased by
yu<u>h</u>ib يحب love, to
yu<u>h</u>ib يحب care for, love
yuhiin يهين insult someone, to
yuhiin يهين offend
yu'iid يعيد return, give back
yu'iid يعيد repeat, to
yu'iir يعير lend, to
yu'jab bi يعجب بـ admire, to
yujaffif يجفف dry, to
yujahhiz يجهز ready, to make
yujammi' يجمع gather, to
yujarrib يجرب try, to
yujarrib يجرب taste, to (sample)
yujarrib يجرب experience, to
yujbir يجبر force, compel
yujiib يجيب answer, to respond (spoken)
yujiib يجيب answer, to respond (written)
yujiid يجيد fluent (excel at)
yukabbir يكبر enlarge, to
yu<u>kh</u>abbi' يخبئ hide, to
yu<u>kh</u>affif يخفف lessen, reduce
yu<u>kh</u>affif يخفف reduce, to

ARABIC–ENGLISH

yukhammin يخمن guess, to
yukhattit يخطط plan, to
yukhayyit يخيط sew, to
yukhbir يخبر let someone know, to
yukhbir يخبر report, to
yukhbir يخبر tell, to (let know)
yukmil يكمل continue, to
yulaa'im يلائم fit, to
yulaahiz يلاحظ notice, to
yulammi' يلمع polish, to
yulawwih يلوح wave, to
yu'lim يعلم inform, to
yu'lin يعلن reveal, to (make known)
yulqii khitaab يلقي خطاب speech, to make a
yumazziq يمزق tear, to rip
yumkin يمكن can, may
yumsik يمسك hold, to grasp
yumsik يمسك catch, to
yunaaqish يناقش discuss, to
yunaaqish يناقش argue, to
yunaasib يناسب measure out, to suit
yunabbih ينبه warn, to
yunazzif ينظف brush, to
yunazzif ينظف clean, to
yunazzim ينظم arrange, to
yunazzim ينظم organise, arrange
yunbuu' ينبوع spring (of water)
yunhii ينهي finish
yunqidh ينقذ rescue, to
yantan ينتن stink, to
yuqaamir يقامر gamble
yuqaarin يقارن compare, to
yuqabbil يقبل kiss, to
yuqaddim talab يقدم طلب apply, to (for permission)
yuqaddim يقدم bring up (topic)
yuqaddim يقدم present, to
yuqaddir يقدر count, reckon
yuqaddir يقدر estimate, to
yuqaddir يقدر value, to
yuqarrir يقرر decide, to
yuqashshir يقشر peel, to
yuqassim يقسم divide, split up
yuqattib يقطب frown, to
yuqill يقل pick up, to (someone)
yuraafiq يرافق accompany, to
yuraasil 'iliktruniyyan يراسل إلكترونيا email, to
yurabbi يربي bring up (children)
yurabbii يربي raise, to (children)
yurahhib يرحب welcome, to
yurakhkhis يرخص permit, to allow
yurakkib يركب assemble, put together
yurakkiz يركز concentrate, to
yurattib يرتب tidy up
yurbik يربك confuse, to
yuriid يريد want, to
yurshid يرشد instruct, tell to do something
yursil faax يرسل فاكس fax, to
yursil يرسل send, to
yursil يرسل mail, to
yusaafir يسافر travel, to
yusaa'id يساعد assist, to
yusaa'id يساعد help, to
yusaamih يسامح forgive, to
yusaawim يساوم bargain, to
yusaddir يصدر export, to
yusaffi يصفي defecate, to
yusahhih يصحح correct, to
yusajjil يسجل register, to
yusajjil يسجل videotape, to
yusakhkhin يسخن heat, to

Y

ARABIC–ENGLISH

Y

yusallii يصلي pray, to
yusallim يسلم greet, to
yusallim يسلم say hello
yusallim يسلم deliver, to
yusallim يسلم hand over
yusarrih يصرح express, state
yusawwi يسوي level (even, flat)
yusawwir يصور photograph, to
yusbih يصبح become, to
yushaahid يشاهد view, look at
yushaahid يشاهد watch, look, see
yushaahid يشاهد watch, to (show, movie)
yushaarik يشارك participate, to
yushaghil يشغل on: to turn something on
yushakkil يشكل shape, to form
yushbih يشبه look like
yushbih يشبه resemble
yushfa يشفى better, get (be cured)
yush'il يشعل switch on, turn on
yush'il يشعل turn on, to
yuslih يصلح mend, to
yuslih يصلح repair, to
yuslih يصلح fix, to (repair)
yutaalib يطالب urge, to push for
yutaarid يطارد chase, to
yutalliq يطلق divorce, to
yutammim يتمم complete, to
yutarjim يترجم translate, to
yutfi' يطفئ off: to turn something off
yutfi' يطفئ turn off, to
yuthaqqif يثقف educate, to
yuthbit يثبت prove, to
yu'ti يعطي give, to
yu'ti يعطي hand out
yutii' يطيع obey, to
yut'im يطعم feed, to
yutliq an-naar يطلق النار shoot, to
yutliq saraah يطلق سراح release, to
yuuqif as-sayyaara يوقف السيارة park, to (car)
yuuqif يوقف stop, to halt
yuuqif يوقف stall, to (car)
yuuqiz يوقظ wake someone up
yuuqiz يوقظ awaken, wake someone up
yuwaafiq يوافق agree, to
yuwaajih يواجه face, to
yuwaasil يواصل stick to, to
yuwaddi' يودع say goodbye
yuwajjih يوجه guide, lead
yuwajjih يوجه steer, to
yuwaqqi' يوقع sign, to
yuwarrid يورد import, to
yuwarrit يورط involve, to
yuwassi' يوسع expand, grow larger
yuzahhir يظهر develop, to (film)
yuzayyin يزين decorate, to
yuzhir يظهر show, to
yuzii' يذيع to broadcast
yuz'ij يزعج bother, disturb
yuz'ij يزعج disturb, to

Z

zaa'id زائد plus
zaa'if زائف false (imitation)
zaara makaanan maa زار مكانا ما have been somewhere
zaawiya زاوية corner

zahra زهرة flower
zahrii زهري pink (rose)
z̲ahr ظهر back (part of body)
zalaabia زلابية dumpling
zamiil زميل colleague, co-worker
zamiil زميل co-worker, colleague
zanjabiil زنجبيل ginger
zawj زوج husband
zawj زوج partner (spouse)
zawja زوجة wife
zawjatu l-'akh زوجة الأخ sister-in-law
zayt as-simsim زيت السمسم sesame oil
zayt زيت oil
zayy زي style
zifaaf زفاف wedding
z̲ifr ظفر nail (finger, toe)
ziina زينة ornament
z̲ill ظل shade
zilzaal زلزال earthquake
ziyaada زيادة increase
ziyaara زيارة visit
zubda زبدة butter
z̲uhr ظهر midday
z̲uhr ظهر noon
zujaaj زجاج glass (material)
zukaam زكام cold, flu
zunbarak زنبرك spring (metal part)

English–Arabic

A

abdomen بطن batn
able to يستطيع yastatii'
about (approximately) تقريبا taqriiban
about (regarding) بخصوص bikhusuus
above, upstairs فوق fawq
abroad خارج البلد khaarij al-balad
absent غائب ghaa'ib
accept, to يقبل yaqbal
accident حادث haadith
accidentally, by chance صدفة sudfatan
accommodation سكن sakan
accompany, to يرافق yuraafiq
according to بالنسبة إلى binnisbati ilaa
accuse, to يتهم yattahim
ache ألم 'alam
ache, to يتوجع yatawajja'
acquaintance إطلاع 'ittilaa'
acquainted, to be مطلع على muttali' 'ala
across عبر 'abra
across from من جانب min jaanib
act, to يفعل yaf'al
action عمل 'amal
activity نشاط nashaat
actually في الواقع fi l-waaqi'
add, to يضيف yudiif
address عنوان 'unwaan
admire, to يعجب بـ yu'jab bi.. (passive)
admit, confess يعترف ya'tarif
adult راشد raashid
advance, go forward يتقدم yataqaddam
advance money, deposit تسبقة tasbiqa
advice نصيحة nasiiha
advise, to ينصح yansah
aeroplane طائرة taa'ira
affect, to يؤثر في yu'athir fi
affection حنان hanaan
afford, to يقدر على yaqdir 'alaa
afraid خائف khaa'if
after بعد ba'da
afternoon (midday) الظهر az-zuhr
afternoon (3pm to dusk) بعد الظهر ba'da az-zuhr
afterwards, then بعد ئذ ba'da 'idhin
again من جديد min jadiid
age عمر 'umr
ago منذ mundhu
agree, to يوافق yuwaafiq
agreed! متفق عليه muttafaq 'alayh
agreement إتفاق ittifaaq
air هواء hawaa'
air conditioning مكيف الهواء mukayyif alhawaa'
airmail بريد جوي bariid jawwy
airplane طائرة taa'ira
airport مطار mataar
alcohol, liquor كحول kuhuul
alike متشابه mutashaabih
a little القليل al-qaliil
alive حي hayy
all كل kull
alley, lane ممشى mamsha
allow, permit يسمح yasmah
allowed to, مسموح ان masmuuh an

almost تقريبا taqriiban
alone وحيد wahiid
a lot الكثير al-kathiir
already بعد ba'du
also أيضا aydan
altogether, in total جميعا jamii'an
although مع ان ma'a 'anna
always دائما daa'iman
ambassador سفير safiir
America امريكا amariica
American اميركي amariikiyy
among بين bayna
amount كمية kammiyya
ancestor سلف salaf
ancient قديم qadiim
and و wa
anger غضب ghadab
angry غاضب ghaadib
animal حيوان hayawaan
ankle كاحل kaahil
annoyed منزعج munza'ij
another (different) مختلف mukhtalif
another (same again) آخر 'aakhar
annual سنوي sanawi
answer, response (spoken) جواب jawaab
answer, response (written) جواب jawaab
answer, to respond (spoken) يجيب yujiib
answer, to respond (written) يجيب yujiib
answer the phone يرد على الهاتف yarudd 'ala l-haatif
answering machine, جهاز الرد الآلي jihaaz ar-rad al'aaliy
antiques الأشياء العتيقة al-ashyaa' al-'atiiqa
anus الشرج ash-sharaj
anybody, anyone أي شخص 'ayyu shakhsin
anything أي شيء ayyu shay'in
anywhere أي مكان ayyu makaanin
ape قرد qird
apart منعزل mun'azil
apartment شقة shaqqa
apologise, to يعتذر ya'tadhir
apparently بوضوح biwuduuh
appear, become visible يظهر yazhar
appearance, looks مظهر mazhar
apple تفاحة tuffaahah
appliance, electrical أداة adaat
apply, to (for permission) يقدم طلب yuqaddim talab
appointment موعد maw'idd
approach, to (in space) يقترب yaqtarib
approach, to (in time) يدنو yadnu
appropriate متوافق mutawaafiq
approximately تقريبا taqriiban
April نيسان naysaan
architecture فن العمارة fann al-'imara
area مساحة masaaha
argue, to يناقش yunaaqish
argument مناقشة munaaqasha
arm ذراع dhiraa'
armchair أريكة ariika
army جيش jaysh
around (approximately) تقريبا taqriiban
around (nearby) قريب qariib
around (surrounding) حول hawla
arrange, to ينظم yunazzim
arrangements, planning مخططات mukhattataat

A

ENGLISH–ARABIC

B

ENGLISH–ARABIC

arrival وصول wu<u>s</u>uul
arrive, to يصل ya<u>s</u>il
art فن fann
article (in newspaper) مقال maqaal
artificial اصطناعي 'i<u>s</u>tinaa'i
artist فنان fannaan
ashamed, embarrassed خجلان <u>kh</u>ajlaan
Asia آسيا aasiya
ask about, to يسال yas'al
ask for, request يطلب ya<u>t</u>lub
asleep نائم naa'im
assemble, gather يجمع yajma'
assemble, put together يركب yurakkib
assist, to يساعد yusaa'id
assistance مساعدة musaa'ada
astonished مندهش mundahi<u>sh</u>
as well أيضا ay<u>d</u>an
at عند 'inda
at home في fii
atmosphere, ambience الجو al-jaw
at night في المساء fii l-masaa'
at once حالا <u>h</u>aalan
attack (in war) هجوم hujuum
attack (with words) تهجم tahajjum
attain, reach يبلغ yablu<u>gh</u>
attempt محاولة mu<u>h</u>aawala
attempt, to يحاول yu<u>h</u>aawil
attend, to يحضر ya<u>h</u>dur
at the latest, آخر اجل aa<u>kh</u>ar ajal
attitude موقف mawqif
attractive جذاب ja<u>dh</u>aab
aubergine, eggplant باذنجان baa<u>dh</u>injaan
auction, to يبيع بالمزاد العلني yabii' bil-mazaad l-'alani
auctioned off يبيع بالمزاد العلني mubaa' bil-mazaad l-'alani
August آب aab
aunt خالة/عمة <u>kh</u>aala / 'amma
Australia استراليا austraaliya
Australian استرالي austraaliy
authority (person in charge) مسؤول mas'uul
authority (power) سلطة sul<u>t</u>a
automobile, car سيارة sayyaara
autumn خريف <u>kh</u>ariif
available موجود mawjuud
available, to make متاح mutaa<u>h</u>
average (numbers) معدل mu'addal
average (so-so, just okay) عادي 'aadii
awake يقظ yaqi<u>z</u>
awake, wake up يستيقظ yastayqi<u>z</u>
awaken, wake someone up يوقظ yuuqi<u>z</u>
aware مدرك mudrik
awareness ادراك 'idraak

B

baby طفل <u>t</u>ifl
back, rear الخلف al-<u>kh</u>alf
back (part of body) ظهر <u>z</u>ahr
back, to go يرجع yarji'
back up, to يدعم yad'am
backward عكسي 'aksii
bad سيء sayyi'
bad luck حظ سيء <u>h</u>a<u>z</u> sayyi'
bag محفظة mi<u>h</u>fa<u>z</u>a
baggage امتعة 'amti'a
bake, to يخبز ya<u>kh</u>biz
baked مخبوز ma<u>kh</u>buuz
bald اصلع a<u>s</u>la'
ball كرة kura
banana موز mawz
bandage ضمادة <u>d</u>ammaada

bank (finance) مصرف masrif
bank (of river) منحدر munhadar
banquet مأدبة ma'duba
bar (blocking way) عائق 'aa'iq
bar (serving drinks) مشرب mashrab
barber حلاق hallaaq
barely بشق الأنفس bishiq al-anfus
bargain, to يساوم yusaawim
barren قاحل qaahil
base, foundation أساس 'asaas
based on على أساس 'alaa asaas
basic أساسي 'asaasi
basis أساس 'asaas
basket سلة salla
basketball كرة السلة kurat as-salla
bath مغطس maghtas
bathe, take a bath يستحم yastahim
bathe, swim يسبح yasbah
bathrobe برنس حمام burnus hammaam
bathroom حمام hammaam
battle معركة ma'raka
bay خليج khaliij
be, exist يكون yakuun
beach بحر bahir
bean فول fuul
beard لحية lihya
beat (to defeat) يغلب yaghlib
beat (to strike) يسحق yashaq
beautiful (of people) وسيم wasiim
beautiful (of places) جميل jamiil
beautiful (of things) جميل jamiil
because لأن li'anna
become, to يصبح yusbih
bed سرير sariir
bedding, bedclothes شراشف sharaashif
bedroom غرفة النوم ghurfat an-nawm
bedsheet شراشف sharaashif
beef لحم البقر lahm al-baqar
beer بيرة biira
before (in time) قبل qabla
before (in front of) أمام amaama
beforehand, earlier مقدما muqaddaman
begin, to يبدأ yabda'
beginning بداية bidaaya
behave يتصرف yatasarraf
behind وراء waraa'
belief, faith إيمان 'iimaan
believe, to يؤمن yu'min
belongings ممتلكات mumtalakaat
belong to ينتمي yantami
below, downstairs تحت taht
belt حزام hizaam
beside وراء waraa'
besides عدا 'ada
best أفضل 'afdal
best wishes أفضل الأمنيات 'afdal al-umniyaat
better أحسن ahsan
better, get (improve) يتحسن yatahassan
better, get (be cured) يشفى yushfa
between بين bayna
bicycle دراجة darraaja
big كبير kabiir
bill فاتورة faatuura
billion بليون balyuun
bird عصفور 'asfuur
birth, to give تلد talid
birthday عيد ميلاد 'iid miilaad

biscuit (salty, cracker) بسكويت baskawiit
biscuit (sweet, cookie) بسكويت baskawiit
bit (part) جزء juzi'
bit (slightly) قليلا qaliilan
bite, to يعض ya'udd
bitter مر murr
black أسود 'aswad
black beans فول أسود fuul 'aswad
blame, to يلوم yaluum
bland رقيق raqiiq
blanket بطانية battaaniya
blind أعمى a'ma
blood دم damm
blouse قميص qamiis
blue أزرق 'azraq
board, to (bus, train) يركب yarkab
boat مركب markab
body جسد jasad
boil, to يغلي yaghlii
boiled مغلي maghli
bone عظم 'azm
bon voyage! رحلة سعيدة rihla sa'iida
book كتاب kitaab
border, edge طرف taraf
border (between countries) حدود huduud
bored ضجر dajir
boring مضجر mudjir
born, to be مولود mawluud
borrow, to يستعير yasta'iir
boss رئيس ra'iis
botanic gardens حدائق نباتية hadaa'iq nabaatiya
both كلا kilaa
both...and معا ma'an
bother, disturb يزعج yuz'ij
bother, disturbance انزعاج 'inzi'aaj
bottle قنينة qanniina
bottom (base) قاعدة qaa'ida
bottom (buttocks), كفل kafal
boundary, border حدود huduud
bowl طبق tabaq
box صندوق sunduuq
box (cardboard) علبة 'ulba
boy صبي sabiyy
boyfriend صديق sadiiq
bra صدرية للثديين sidriya lil-thadyayn
bracelet سوار siwaar
brain دماغ dimaagh
brake, مكبح mikbah
brake, to يكبح yakbah
branch غصن ghusn
brave, daring شجاع shujaa'
bread خبز khubz
break, shatter كسر kasr
break apart, to يكسر yaksir
break down, to (car, machine) يتعطل yata'attal
breakfast, morning meal فطور fatuur
breakfast, to eat يتناول الفطور yatanaawal al-fatuur
breasts ثدي thadyi
bride عروس 'aruus
bridegroom عريس 'ariis
bridge جسر jisir
brief مختصر mukhtasar
briefcase حقيبة haqiiba
briefs مختصر mukhtasar
bright ساطع saati'
bring, to يجلب yajlib
bring up (topic) يقدم yuqaddim
bring up (children) يربي yurabbi
British بريطاني briitaani
broad, spacious واسع waasi'
broadcast, program برنامج barnaamaj

broadcast, to يذيع yudhii’
broccoli البركولي al-barkuuli
broken, does not work, spoiled مكسور maksuur
broken, shattered محطم muhattam
broken, snapped (of bones, etc.) مكسور maksuur
broken off مكسور maksuur
bronze البرونز al-brunz
broom مكنسة miknasa
broth, soup حساء hisaa’
brother أخ ’akh
brother-in-law صهر sihr
brown بني bunni
bruise رضة radda
brush فرشاة furshaat
brush, to ينظف yunazzif
bucket دلو dalu
Buddhism البوذية al-buudhiya
Buddhist بوذي buudzi
buffalo (water buffalo) جاموس jamuus
build, to يبني yabni
building مبنى mabnaa
burn (injury) حرق harq
burn, to يحرق yahriq
burned down, out محروق mahruuq
Burma بورما burma
Burmese بورمي burmii
bus حافلة/باص haafila / baas
bus station محطة الباص mahattat l-baas
business عمل ’amal
businessperson رجل أعمال rajul a’maal
busy (doing something) مشغول mashghuul
busy (crowded) مزدحم muzdahim
busy (telephone) مشغول mashghuul
but لكن laakin
butter زبدة zubda
butterfly فراشة faraasha
buttocks كفل kafal
buy, to يشتري yashtari
by (author, artist) مكتوب بقلم maktuub biqalam
by means of بواسطة biwaasitat
by the way على فكرة ’ala fikra

C

cabbage ملفوف malfuuf
cabbage, Chinese ملفوف صيني malfuuf siinii
cake, pastry كعكة، عجين ka’ka, ’ajiin
calculate يحسب yahsub
calculator آلة حاسبة ’aala haasiba
call, summon يستدعي yastad’ii
call on the telephone يتصل yattasil
called, named مسمى musamma
calm هادئ haadi’
Cambodia كمبوديا kambuudia
Cambodian كمبودي kambuudi
camera آلة تصوير ’aalat taswiir
can, be able to يستطيع yastatii’
can, may يمكن yumkin
can, tin علبة معدنية ’ulba ma’daniya
cancel يلغي yulghi
candle شمعة sham’a
candy, sweets حلوى halwa
capable of, to be مؤهل mu’ahhal
capture, to يقبض على yaqbid ’ala
car, automobile سيارة sayyara
cardboard كرتون kartuun

C

ENGLISH–ARABIC

cards, game لعبة ورق lub'at waraq
care for, love يحب yuhib
care of, to take يهتم بـ yahtam bi
careful! إحذر ihdhar
carpet سجادة sajjaada
carrot جزر jazar
carry, to يحمل yahmil
cart (horsecart) عربة 'araba
cart (pushcart) عربة 'araba
carve, to ينحت yanhat
carving نحت nahit
cash, money مال maal
cash a check, to يحول إلى نقد yuhawwil 'ila naqid
cassette شريط shariit
cat هر، قطة hirr; qitta
catch, to يمسك yumsik
cauliflower قرنبيط qarnabiit
cause سبب sabab
cautious حذر hadhir
cave كهف kahif
CD القرص المضغوط al-qurs al-madghuut
CD-ROM محرك الأقراص muharrik l-aqraas
ceiling سقف saqf
celebrate, to يحتفل yahtafil
celery الكرفس al-karfas
cell phone هاتف نقال haatif naqqaal
centre, middle وسط wasat
centre (of city) وسط wasat
central مركزي markaziy
century قرن qarin
ceremony مراسم maraasim
certain, sure أكيد 'akiid
certainly! طبعا tab'an
certificate شهادة shahaada
chair كرسي kursi
challenge تحدي tahaddi
champion بطل batal
chance, opportunity فرصة fursa
chance, by بالصدفة bis-sudfa
change, small تغيير بسيط taghyiir basiit
change, to (conditions, situations) يغيير yughayyir
change, exchange (money) تصريف tasriif
change, switch (clothes) يغير yughayyir
change one's mind يغير رأية yughayyir ra'yahu
character (personality) شخصية shakhsiya
character (written) حرف harf
characteristic مميز mumayyaz
chase, to يطارد yutaarid
chase away, chase out يطرد yatrud
cheap رخيص rakhiis
cheat, to يغش yaghish
cheat, someone who cheats غشاش ghashash
check, verify يفحص yafhas
checked (pattern) مربعات murabba'aat
cheek خد khadd
cheers! بصحتك bisihhatik
cheese جبن jubn
chess شطرنج shatranj
chest (box) صندوق sunduuq
chest (breast) صدر sadir
chew, to يمضغ yamdagh
chicken دجاج dajaaj
child (young person) طفل tifl
child (offspring) ابن ibn
chilli pepper فلفل fulful
chilli sauce صلصة الفلفل salsat al-fulful
chilled مثلج muthallaj

chin ذقن dhaqin
China الصين as-siin
Chinese صيني siinii
chocolate شوكولا shukulaa
choice خيار khayaar
choose, to يختار yakhtaar
chopsticks العودان al-'uudaan
Christian مسيحي masiihiyy
Christianity الديانة المسيحية al-diyaana al-masiihiyya
church كنيسة kaniisa
cigar سيكار siikaar
cigarette سيكارة siikaara
cilantro, coriander كزبرة kuzbara
cinema سنيما siinama
circle دائرة daa'ira
citizen مواطن muwaatin
citrus ليمون laymuun
city مدينة madiina
class, category درجة daraja
classes (at university) صفوف sufuuf
clean نظيف naziif
clean, to ينظف yunazzif
cleanliness نظافة nazaafa
clear (of weather) مشرق mushriq
clever ذكي dhakii
climate طقس taqs
climb onto, into يصعد yas'ad
climb up (hills, mountains) يتسلق yatasallaq
clock ساعة saa'a
close together, tight ضيق dayyiq
close to, nearby قريب qariib
close, to cover يغطي yughatti
closed (door) مغلق mughlaq
closed (shop) مقفل muqfal
closed (road) مقطوع maqtuu'
cloth قماش qumaash
clothes, clothing ثياب thiyaab
cloudy, overcast غائم ghaa'im
clove cigarette ورق السجائر waraq as-sajaa'ir
cloves فصوص fusuus
coat, jacket سترة sutra
coat, overcoat معطف mi'taf
coconut جوز الهند jawz al-hind
coffee قهوة qahwa
coin نقد معدني naqd ma'dani
cold برد bard
cold, flu زكام zukaam
colleague, co-worker زميل zamiil
collect payment, to يقبض yaqbad
collide, to يتصادم yatasaadam
collision تصادم tasaadum
colour لون lawn
comb مشط musht
come, to يأتي ya'tii
come back يرجع yarja'
come in يدخل yadkhul
come on, let's go هيّا hayyaa
comfortable مرتاح murtaah
command, order أمر 'amr
command, to يأمر ya'mur
common, frequent عادي 'aadii
company, firm شركة sharika
compare, to يقارن yuqaarin
compared with بالمقارنة مع bil-muqaarana ma'a
compete, to يتنافس yatanaafas
competition منافسة munaafasa
complain, to يتذمر yatadhammar
complaint شكوى shakwa
complete (whole) كامل kaamil
complete (thorough) شامل shaamil
complete (finished) متمم mutammam

C

ENGLISH–ARABIC

complete, to يتمم yutammim
completely تماماً tamaaman
complicated معقد mu'aqqad
compose, write (letters, books, music) يكتب yaktub
composition, writings مؤلفات mu'allafaat
compulsory إجباري 'ijbaarii
computer حاسوب haasuub
concentrate, to يركز yurakkiz
concerning بالنسبة إلى bin-nisba 'ila
condition (pre-condition) شرط shart
condition (status) حالة haala
confectionery حلويات halawiyaat
confidence ثقة thiqa
confidence, to have يثق yathiq
Confucianism الكونفوشيوسية al-kunfuushiyusiyya
confuse, to يربك yurbik
confused (in a mess) مرتبك murtabik
confused (mentally) مشوش mushawwash
confusing مربك murbik
congratulations! تهانينا tahaaniina
connect together, to يرتبط yartabit
conscious of, to be مدرك mudrik
consider (to have an opinion) يعتقد ya'taqid
consider (to think over) يفكر yufakkir
consult, talk over with يستشير yastashiir
contact, connection صلة sila
contact, get in touch with يتصل yattasil
continent قارة qaarra
continue, to يكمل yukmil
convenient مناسب munaasib
conversation حديث hadiith
cook (person) طباخ tabbaakh
cook, to يطبخ yatbukh
cooked مطبوخ matbuukh
cooker, stove جهاز للطبخ jihaz lit-tabkh
cookie, sweet biscuit كعكة محلاة ka'ka muhallaat
cooking, cuisine طبخ tabkh
cool فاتر faatir
cool, to يبرد yabrud
copper نحاس nuhaas
copy نسخة nuskha
coral مرجان murjaan
coriander, cilantro كزبرة kuzbara
corn, grain ذرة dhura
corner زاوية zaawiya
correct صح sahh
correct, to يصحح yusahhih
correspond (write letters) يتراسل yataraasal
corridor رواق riwaaq
cost (expense) كلفة kulfa
cost (price) ثمن thaman
cotton قطن qutn
couch, sofa أريكة 'ariika
cough سعال su'aal
cough, to يسعل yas'ul
could, might يستطيع yastatii'
count, reckon يقدر yuqaddir
counter (for paying, buying tickets) نافذة التذاكر naafidhat at-tadhaakir
country (nation) بلد balad
country (rural area) ريف riif
courgettes, zucchini كوسا kuusaa
courtyard ساحة الدار saahat ad-dar

cover, to يغطي yughatti
cow بقرة baqara
co-worker, colleague زميل zamiil
crab سرطان sarataan
cracked مكسور maksuur
cracker, salty biscuit بسكويتة مالحة baskawiita maaliha
crafts حرف hiraf
craftsperson حرفي hirafii
crate قفص qafas
crazy مجنون majnuun
create, to يخلق yakhliq
criminal مجرم mujrim
cross, angry غاضب ghaadib
cross, go over يعبر ya'bur
crowded مزدحم muzdahim
cruel قاس qaasin
cry, to يبكي yabki
cry out, to يصرخ yasrukh
cucumber خيار khiyaar
cuisine, style of cooking اسلوب طبخ 'usluub tabikh
culture حضارة hadaara
cup كوب kuub
cupboard خزانة khizaana
cure (medical) دواء dawaa'
cured, preserved معقم mu'aqqam
currency عملة 'umla
curtain ستارة sitaara
custom, tradition عادة 'aada
cut, slice قطعة qit'a
cut, to يقص yaquss
cute, appealing جذاب jadhdhaab

D

daily يوميا yawmiyyan
damage ضرر darar
damage, to يضر yadurr
damp رطب ratib
dance رقصة raqsa
dance, to يرقص yarqus
danger خطر khatar
dangerous خطير khatiir
dark مظلم muzlim
date (of the month) تاريخ taariikh
date of birth تاريخ الميلاد taariikh al-miilaad
daughter ابنة 'ibna
daughter-in-law الكنة al-kanna
dawn فجر fajir
day يوم yawm
day after tomorrow بعد الغد ba'da l-ghad
day before yesterday امس الأول amsi al-awwal
daydream, to يستغرق في أحلام اليقظة yastaghriq fi ahlaam al-yaqaza
day off عطلة 'utla
day of the week يوم yawm
dead ميت mayyit
deaf أصم 'asamm
death موت mawt
debt دين dayn
deceive, to يخدع yakhda'
December كانون الأول kaanuun al-awwal
decide, to يقرر yuqarrir
decision قرار qaraar
decline (get less) ينخفض yankhafid
decline (refuse) يرفض yarfud
decorate, to يزين yuzayyin
decrease, to ينقص yanqus
deep عميق 'amiiq
defeat, to يهزم yahzim
defecate, to يصفي yusaffi
defect خلل khalal
defend (in war) يحمي yahmi
defend (with words) يدافع yudaafi'

D

ENGLISH–ARABIC

definite محدد muhaddad
degree, level درجة daraja
degrees (temperature) درجة daraja
delay تأخير ta'khiir
delayed متأخر muta'akhkhir
delicious لذيذ ladhiidh
deliver, to يسلم yusallim
demand, to يطلب yatlub
depart, to يرحل yarhal
department شقة shaqqa
department store محل mahal
departure رحيل rahiil
depend on, to يعتمد على ya'tamid 'ala
deposit (leave behind with someone) أمانة amaana
deposit (put money in the bank) وديعة wadii'a
descendant هابط haabit
describe, to يصف yasif
desert (arid land) صحراء sahraa'
desert, to abandon يترك yatruk
desire رغبة raghba
desire, to يرغب yarghab
desk مكتب maktab
dessert حلوى halwa
destination المكان المقصود al-makaan al-maqsuud
destroy, to يحطم yuhattim
destroyed, ruined محطم muhattam
detergent منظف munazzif
determined, stubborn عنيد 'aniid
develop, to (happen) ينشأ yansha'
develop, to (film) يظهر yuzahhir
development تطور tatawwur
diagonal قطري qutrii
diagonally خط قطري khat qutriyy
dial, to (telephone) يتصل yattasil
dialect لهجة lahja
diamond الماس almaas
diary, daybook دفتر لتدوين اليوميات daftar litadwiin al-yawmiyyaat
diary, journal مذكرة mudhakkara
dictionary قموس qaamuus
die, to يموت yamuut
difference (discrepancy in figures) اختلاف 'ikhtilaaf
difference (in quality) اختلاف 'ikhtilaaf
different, other مختلف mukhtalif
difficult صعب sa'b
dinner, evening meal عشاء 'ashaa'
dinner, to eat يتناول العشاء yatanaawal al-'ashaa'
dipper, ladle مغرفة mighrafa
direction ادارة 'idara
director (of company) مدير mudiir
dirt, filth قذارة qadhaara
dirty قذر qadhir
disappointed مخيب mukhayyab
disaster كارثة kaaritha
discount خصم khasim
discover, to يكتشف yaktashif
discuss, to يناقش yunaaqish
discussion مناقشة munaaqasha
disease داء daa'
disgusting مقرف muqrif
dish, platter صحن sahn
dish (particular food) طبق tabaq
diskette قرص qirs
dislike, to يكره yakrah

display عرض ’ard
display, to يعرض ya’rud
distance مسافة masaafa
disturb, to يزعج yuz’ij
disturbance ازعاج ‘iz’aaj
divide, split up يقسم yuqassim
divided by مقسوم على maqsuum ’ala
divorce, to يطلق yutalliq
divorced مطلق mutallaq
do, perform an action يفعل yaf’al
don’t! لاتفعل ذلك laa taf’al dhaalik
don’t mention it! العفو al’afw
do one’s best حاول قدر المستطاع haawil qadra al-mustataa’
doctor طبيب tabiib
document, letter رسالة risaala
dog كلب kalb
done (cooked) جاهز jaahiz
done (finished) منجز munjaz
door باب baab
double مزدوج muzdawij
doubt, to يشك yashukk
down, downward تحت tahta
downstairs الطابق الأسفل at-taabiq al-asfal
downtown وسط المدينة wasat al-madiina
dozen دزينة dazzina
draw, to يرسم yarsum
drawer رسام rassaam
drawing رسم rasim
dream حلم hilm
dream, to يحلم yahlum
dress, frock ثوب thawb
dressed, to get يلبس yalbas
drink, refreshment شراب sharaab
drink, to يشرب yashrab
drive, to (a car) يسوق yasuuq
drought جفاف jafaaf
drown, to يغرق yaghraq
drug (medicine) دواء dawaa’
drug (recreational) مخدر mukhaddir
drugstore, pharmacy صيدلية saydaliyya
drunk سكران sakraan
dry جاف jaaf
dry (weather) جاف jaaf
dry, to يجفف yujaffif
dry out (in the sun) يجف yajiff
duck بطة batta
dull (boring) مضجر mudjir
dull (weather) غائم ghaa’im
dumpling زلابية zalaabia
during خلال khilaal
dusk مظلم muzlim
dust غبار ghubaar
duty (import tax) رسم rasm
duty (responsibility) واجب waajib
DVD الدي في دي ad-dii fii dii

E

each, every كل kull
ear أذن ‘udhun
earrings حلق halaq
earlier, beforehand قبل qabil
early مبكر mubkir
early in the morning صباحا sabaahan
earn, to يجني yajni
earth, soil تراب turaab
Earth, the world أرض ard
earthquake زلزال zilzaal
east شرق sharq
easy سهل sahil
eat, to يأكل ya’kul
economical اقتصادي ‘iqtisaadii
economy اقتصاد ‘iqtisaad

edge حافة haaffa
educate, to يثقف yuthaqqif
education ثقافة thaqaafa
effect, result نتيجة natiija
effort جهد juhd
effort, to make an يقوم بجهد yaquum bijuhd
egg بيضة bayda
eggplant, aubergine باذنجان baadhinjaan
eight ثمانية thamaaniya
eighteen ثمانية عشر thamaaniyata 'ashara
eighty ثمانين thamaaniin
either أي من ayy min
elbow مرفق mirfaq
elder أكبر سنا akbara sinnan
election انتخابات 'intikhaabaat
electric كهربائي kahrubaa'ii
electricity كهرباء kahrubaa'
electronic إلكتروني 'iliktrunii
elegant أنيق 'aniiq
elephant فيل fiil
elevator مصعد mis'ad
eleven احد عشر ahada 'ashara
else: anything else آخر aakhar
else: or else آخر aakhar
email (system) بريد إلكتروني bariid 'iliktrunii
email (message) رسالة إلكترونية risaala 'iliktruniya
email, to يراسل إلكترونيا yuraasil 'iliktruniyyan
email address عنوان إلكتروني 'unwaan 'iliktrunii
embarrassed خجلان khajlaan
embarrassing مخجل mukhjil
embassy سفارة safaara
embrace, to يعانق yu'aaniq
embroidered مطرز mutarraz
embroideryb تطريز tatriiz
emergency طوارئ tawaari'
emotion عاطفة 'aatifa
empty فارغ faarigh
end (tip) طرف taraf
end (finish) نهاية nihaaya
end, to ينتهي yantahi
enemy عدو 'aduw
energy طاقة taaqa
engaged (telephone) مشغول mashghuul
engaged (to be married) خاطب khaatib
engine محرك muharrik
England إنكلترا 'inkiltra
English إنكليزي 'inkliizii
engrave, to ينقش yanqush
enjoy, to يستمتع yastamti'
enjoyable ممتع mumti'
enjoy oneself, to يستمتع yastamti'
enlarge, to يكبر yukabbir
enough كاف kafin
enquire, to يسأل yas'al
enter, to يدخل yadkhul
entire كل kull
entirety, whole مجموع majmuu'
entrance, way in مدخل madkhal
envelope مغلف mughallaf
envious حسود hasuud
environment, the بيئة bii'a
envy حسد hasad
equal معادل mu'aadil
equality معادلة mu'aadala
error خطأ khata'
escalator سلم متحرك sullam mutaharrik
especially خاصة khaassatan
establish, set up يؤسس yu'assis
essay مقال maqaal
estimate, to يقدر yuqaddir

ethnic group عرق 'irq
Europe أوروبا 'urubba
even (also) حتى hatta
even (smooth) أملس 'amlas
evening مساء masaa'
event حدث hadath
ever, have already دائما daa'iman
every كل kull
everybody, everyone الجميع al-jamii'
every kind of كل نوع kull naw'
everything كل شيء kull shay'
every time كل مرة kull marra
everywhere في كل مكان fii kull makaan
exact, exactly دقيق daqiiq
exactly! just so! تماما tamaaman
exam, test فحص fahis
examine, to يفحص yafhas
example مثل mathal
example, for مثلا mathalan
excellent ممتاز mumtaaz
except ما عدا maa 'adaa
exchange, to (money, opinions) تبادل tabaadul
exchange rate سعر التبادل si'r at-tabaadul
excited متحمس mutahammis
exciting مثير muthiir
excuse me! (attracting attention) عفوان 'afwan
excuse me! (getting past) بالإذن bil'idhn
excuse me! (apology) عفوا 'afwan
exist, to يكون yakuun
exit, way out مخرج makhraj
expand, grow larger يوسع yuwassi'
expect, to يتوقع yatawaqqa'
expense حساب hisaab
expenses مصاريف masaariif
expensive غال ghaalin
experience تجربة tajriba
experience, to يجرب yujarrib
expert خبير khabiir
explain, to يشرح yashrah
export تصدير tasdiir
export, to يصدر yusaddir
express, state يصرح yusarrih
extension (telephone) تمديد tamdiid
extra إضافي 'idaafii
extremely جدا jiddan
eye عين 'ayn
eyebrow حاجب haajib
eyeglasses, spectacles نظارات nazzaaraat

F

fabric, textile قماش qumaash
face وجه wajih
face, to يواجه yuwaajih
fact حقيقة haqiiqa
factory معمل ma'mal
fail, to يفشل yafshal
failure فشل fashal
fall (season) خريف khariif
fall, to يسقط yasqut
fall over يقع yaqa'
false (imitation) زائف zaa'if
false (not true) خطا khata'
family عائلة 'aa'ila
famine مجاعة majaa'a
famous مشهور mashhuur
fan (admirer) معجب mu'jab
fan (for cooling) مروحة mirwaha
fancy فاخر faakhir
far بعيد ba'iid
fare طعام ta'aam

F

ENGLISH–ARABIC

fast, rapid سريع sarii’
fast, to يصوم yasuum
fat, grease دهنيات duhniyyaat
fat, plump سمين samiin
father أب ’abb
father-in-law حمو hamuu
fault غلطة ghalta
fax (machine) فاكس faax
fax (message) فاكس faax
fax, to يرسل فاكس yursil faax
fear خوف khawf
February شباط shubaat
fee رسم rasim
feed, to يطعم yut’im
feel, to يشعر yash’ur
feeling شعور shu’uur
female أنثى ’unthaa
fence سياج siyaaj
ferry الباخرة العبارة al-baakhira al-’abbaara
fertile خصب khasib
festival مهرجان mahrajaan
fetch, to يحضر yuhdir
fever حمى humma
few قليل qaliil
fiancé خطيب khatiib
fiancée خطيبة khatiiba
field, empty space حقل haqil
fierce مفترس muftaris
fifteen خمسة عشر khamsata ’ashar
fifty خمسين khamsiin
fight, to (physically) يتشاجر yatashaajar
fight over, to يتخاصم من اجل yatakhaasam min ajli
figure, number عدد ’adad
fill, to يملأ yamla’
fill out (form) يملأ yamla’
film (camera) فيلم للتصوير الفوتوغرافي film li-taswiir al-futtughraafiyy
film, movie فيلم سينمائي film sinamaa’i
final آخر ’aakhar
finally آخيرا ’akhiiran
find, to يجد yajid
fine (okay) جيد jayyid
fine (punishment) خطية khatiyya
finger إصبع ’isba’
finish ينهي yunhii
finish off, to يقضي على yaqdii ’alaa
finished (complete) كامل kaamil
finished (none left) فارغ faarigh
fire نار naar
fire someone, to يطرد yatrud
fireworks العاب نارية al’aab naariyya
firm, company شركة sharika
firm (mattress) متين matiin
firm (definite) ثابت thaabit
first أول ’awwal
first, earlier, beforehand قبل qabla
fish سمك samak
fish, to يصطاد yastaad
fish paste معجون سمك ma’juun samak
fish sauce صلصة السمك salsat as-samak
fit, to يلائم yulaa’im
fitting, suitable ملائم mulaa’im
five خمسة khamsa
fix, to (a time, appointment) يحدد yuhaddid
fix, to (repair) يصلح yuslih
flag علم ’alam
flashlight, torch ضوء ومضي daw’ wamdii
flat, smooth مسطح musattah
flat, apartment شقة shaqqa

flight طيران tayaraan
flood طوفان tuufaan
floor أرض ard
flour طحين tahiin
flower زهرة zahra
flu زكام zukaam
fluent يجيد yujiid
flute الة النفخ 'aalat an-nafikh
fly (insect) ذبابة dhubaaba
fly, to يطير yatiir
fog ضباب dabaab
fold, to يطوي yatwi
follow along, to يلحق yalhaq
follow behind, to يتبع yatba'
following الموالي al-muwaalii
fond of, to be مغرم mughram
food طعام ta'aam
foot رجل rijil
for لأجل li'ajli
forbid, to يمنع yamna'
forbidden ممنوع mamnuu'
force قوة quwwa
force, compel يجبر yujbir
forehead جبين jabiin
foreigner أجنبي ajnabii
forest غابة ghaaba
for ever للأبد lil'abad
forget about, to ينسى yansa
forget, to ينسى yansa
forgive, to يسامح yusaamih
forgiveness, mercy سماح، رحمة samaah; rahma
forgotten منسي mansii
fork شوكة shawka
form (shape) شكل shakl
form (to fill out) استمارة 'istimaara
fortress حصن hisn
fortunately لحسن الحظ lihusn al-haz
forty أربعين 'arba'iin
forward أمامي 'amaamii
four أربعة 'arba'a
fourteen أربعة عشر 'arba'ata 'ashar
free of charge مجاني majjaanii
free of restraints حر hurr
free, independent مستقل mustaqil
freedom حرية hurriyya
freeze صقيع saqii'
frequent متكرر mutakarrir
fresh طازج taazaj
Friday جمعة jumu'a
fried مقلي maqlii
friend رفيق rafiiq
friendly, outgoing لطيف latiif
frightened خائف khaa'if
from من min
front جبهة jabha
front: in front of أمام amaama
frown عبوس 'abuus
frown, to يقطب yuqattib
frozen متجمد mutajammid
fruit فاكهة faakiha
fry, to يقلي yaqlii
fulfil يحقق yuhaqqiq
full مليء malii'
full, eaten one's fill شبعان shab'aan
fun, to have يتسلى yatasalla
function, to work يعمل ya'mal
funds, funding رأسمال ra'smaal
funeral جنازة janaaza
fungus فطر fitir
funny مضحك mud-hik
furniture أثاث 'athaath
further, additional إضافي idaafii
fussy متطلب mutatallib
future: in future مستقبل mustaqbal

G

gamble يقامر yuqaamir

game لعبة lu'ba
garage (for repairs) ورشة تصليح warshat tasliih
garage (for parking) مرأب mir'aab
garbage نفاية nifaaya
garden, yard حديقة hadiiqa
gardens, park حديقة عامة hadiiqa 'aamma
garlic ثوم thuum
garment ثوب thawb
gasoline بنزين banziin
gasoline station محطة البنزين mahattat al-banziin
gate بوابة bawwaaba
gather, to يجمع yujammi'
gender جنس jins
general, all-purpose عام 'aam
generally عموما 'umuuman
generous كريم kariim
gentle ناعم naa'im
gesture إيماء 'iimaa'
get, receive ينال yanaal
get off (transport) يترجل yatarajjal
get on (transport) يركب yarkab
get up (from bed) ينهض yanhad
get well soon! تمنيات بالشفاء العجال tamanniyaat bi-shifaa' al-'aajil
ghost شبح shabah
gift هدية hadiyya
ginger زنجبيل zanjabiil
girl بنت bint
girlfriend صاحبة saahiba
give, to يعطي yu'ti
given name اسم 'ism
glad سعيد sa'iid
glass (for drinking) كوب kuub
glass (material) زجاج zujaaj
glasses, spectacles نظارات nazzaaraat
glutinous rice ارز لزج 'aruzz lazij
go, to يذهب yadhhab
go along, join in يتعاون yata'aawan
go around, visit يزور yazuur
go back يعود ya'uud
go for a walk يتمشى yatamashsha
go home يعود ya'uud
go out, exit يخرج yakhruj
go out (fire, candle) يطفأ yatfa'
go to bed ينام yanaam
go up, climb يتسلق yatasallaq
goal هدف hadaf
goat ماعز maa'iz
God رب rabb
god إله 'ilaah
goddess الآلهة al'aaliha
gold ذهب dhahab
golf غولف ghulf
gone, finished منتهي muntahii
good جيد jayyid
goodbye إلى اللقاء 'ila l-liqaa'
good luck! حظا سعيدا hazzan sa'iidan
goodness! يا إلهي yaa ilahii
goose وزة wazza
government حكومة hukuuma
gradually تدريجيا tadriijiyyan
grand, great عظيم 'aziim
grandchild حفيد hafiid
granddaughter حفيدة hafiida
grandfather جد jadd
grandmother جدة jadda
grandparents أجداد ajdaad
grandson حفيد hafiid
grapes عنب 'inab
grass عشب 'ushb
grateful ممنون mamnuun
grave قبر qabr

grey رمادي ramaadi
great, impressive عظيم 'aziim
green أخضر akhdar
green beans الفاصوليا الخضراء al-fasuuliya al-khadraa'
greens الخضار al-khudaar
greet, to يسلم yusallim
greetings سلام salaam
grill, to يشوي yashwii
ground, earth أرض ard
group مجموعة majmuu'a
grow, be growing (plant) ينبت yanbut
grow, cultivate يزرع yazra'
grow larger, to يكبر yakbur
grow up (child) يكبر yakbur
guarantee ضمان damaan
guarantee, to يضمن yadman
guard, to يحرس yahrus
guess, to يخمن yukhammin
guest ضيف dayf
guesthouse منزل الضيوف manzil ad-duyuuf
guest of honour ضيف الشرف dayf ash-sharaf
guide, lead يوجه yuwajjih
guidebook دليل daliil
guilty (of a crime) مذنب mudhnib
guilty, to feel يشعر بالذنب yash'ur bidh-dhanb

H

hair شعر sha'r
half نصف nisf
hall ساحة saaha
hand يد yad
handicap معاق mu'aaq
handicraft حرفة hirfa
handle مسكة maska
hand out يعطي yu'ti
hand over يسلم yusallim
handsome وسيم wasiim
hang, to يعلق yu'alliq
happen, occur يحدث yahduth
happened, what happened? حدث hadath
happening, incident حدث hadatha
happy سعيد sa'iid
happy birthday! عيد ميلاد سعيد 'iid miilaad sa'iid
happy new year! كل عام و أنت بخير kullu 'aam wa anta bikhayr
Harbour مرفأ marfa'
hard (difficult) صعب sa'b
hard (solid) قاس qaasin
hard disk القرص الثابت al-qurs ath-thaabit
hardly بصعوبة bisu'uuba
hardworking, industrious مجتهد mujtahid
harmonious متناغم mutanaaghim
hat قبعة qubba'a
hate, to يكره yakrah
hatred كراهية karaahiya
have, own يملك yamluk
have been somewhere زرا مكانا ما zaara makanan maa
have done something فعل شيئا ما fa'ala shay'an maa
have to, must يجب yajib
he, him هو huwa
head رأس ra's
head for, toward يتوجه yatawajjah
headdress غطاء للرأس ghataa' lir-ra's
healthy سليم saliim
hear, to يسمع yasma'
heart قلب qalb
heat, to يسخن yusakhkhin
heavy ثقيل thaqiil

H

ENGLISH–ARABIC

height طول tuul
hello, hi مرحبا marhaban
hello! (on phone) مرحبا marhaban
help! النجدة an-najda
help, to يساعد yusaa'id
her, hers لها lahaa
here هنا huna
hidden مخفي makhfii
hide, to يخبئ yukhabbi'
high عال 'aalin
hill تلة talla
hinder, to يمنع yamna'
hindrance عائق 'aa'iq
hire, to يؤجر yu'ajjir
his له lahu
history تاريخ taariikh
hit, strike ضربة darba
hobby هواية hiwaaya
hold, to grasp يمسك yumsik
hold back يخفي yukhfi
hole حفرة hufra
holiday (festival) عيد 'iid
holiday (vacation) عطلة 'utla
holy مقدس muqaddas
home, house منزل manzil
honest صريح sariih
honey عسل 'asal
Hong Kong هونكوهغ hunkung
hope, to يتأمل yata'ammal
hopefully أملا amalan
horse حصان hisaan
hospital مستشفى mustashfaa
host مضيف mudiif
hot (spicy) حاد haad
hot (temperature) حار haar
hotel فندق funduq
hot spring ربيع ساخن rabii' saakhin
hour ساعة saa'a
house بيت bayt
how? كيف kayfa
how are you? كيف الحال kayfa al-haal
however لكن laakin
how long? إلى متى 'ila mata
how many? كم kamm
how much? كم kamm
how old? كم عمرك kamm 'umruk
huge كبير kabiir
human انسان 'insaan
humid رطب ratib
humorous مضحك mudhik
hundred مئة mi'a
hundred thousand مئة ألف mi'at alf
hungry جائع jaa'i'
hurry up! أسرع asri'
hurt (injured) مجروح majruuh
hurt, to (cause pain) يؤلم yu'lim
husband زوج zawj
hut, shack كوخ kuukh

I

I, me أنا anaa
ice ثلج thalj
ice cream بوظة buuza
idea فكرة fikra
identical مماثل mumaathil
if إذا 'idhaa
ignore, to يتحاشى yatahaasha
ignorant جاهل jaahil
illegal غير قانوني ghayr qaanuuni
ill, sick مريض mariid
illness مرض marad
imagine, to يتخيل yatakhayyal
immediately حالا haalan
impolite غير مهذب ghayr muhadhab
import استيراد 'istiiraad
import, to يورد yuwarrid
importance أهمية 'ahammiyya

important مهم muhim
impossible مستحيل mustahiil
impression, to make an يؤثر yu'aththir
impressive مؤثر mu'aththir
in, at (space) في fii
in (time, years) خلال khilaal
in addition بالإضافة bil'idaafa
incense بخور bakhuur
incident حدث hadath
included, including بما في ذلك bimaa fii dhalika
increase زيادة ziyaada
increase, to يزيد yaziid
indeed! عجبا 'ajaban
indigenous أصلي 'aslii
Indonesia أندونيسيا 'induniisiya
Indonesian أندونيسي 'induniisii
inexpensive رخيص rakhiis
influence تأثير ta'thiir
influence, to يؤثر yu'aththir
inform, to يعلم yu'lim
information معلومات ma'luumaat
information booth صندوق معلومات sunduuq ma'luumaat
inhabitant ساكن saakin
inject, to يحقن yahqun
injection حقنة huqna
injured مجروح majruuh
injury جرح jurh
ink حبر hibr
in order that, so that لكي likay
insane مجنون majnuun
insect حشرة hashara
inside داخل daakhil
inside of بداخل bidaakhil
inspect, to يفحص yafhas
instead of بدل badal
instruct, tell to do something يرشد yurshid
insult إهانة 'ihaana
insult someone, to يهين yuhiin
insurance تأمين ta'miin
intend, to يقصد yaqsid
intended for مقصود maqsuud
intention قصد qasd
interest (paid to/by a bank) فائدة faa'ida
interested in مهتم muhtamm
interesting مهم muhimm
international عالمي 'aalamii
Internet انترنيت 'intirniit
interpreter مترجم mutarjim
intersection تقاطع taqaatu'
into في fii
introduce oneself, to يعرف yu'arrif
introduce someone, to يعرف yu'arrif
invent, to يخترع yakhtari'
invitation دعوة da'wa
invite, to (ask along) يدعو yad'uu
invite, to (formally) يدعو yad'uu
invoice فاتورة faatuura
involve, to يورط yuwarrit
involved متورط mutawarrit
Ireland أيرلندا 'irlandaa
Irish ايرلندي 'irlandii
iron حديد hadiid
iron, to (clothing) يكوي yakwii
Islam إسلام 'islaam
island جزيرة jaziira
item, individual thing قطعة qit'a
ivory عاج 'aaj

J

jacket سترة sutra
jail سجن sijn
jam معجون ma'juun
January كانون الثاني kanuun ath-thaanii

J

ENGLISH-ARABIC

Japan اليابان al-yaabaan
Japanese ياباني yaabaani
jaw فك fakk
jealous غيور ghayyuur
jealousy غيرة ghiira
jewellery مجوهرات mujawharaat
job عمل 'amal
join together, to يصل yasil
join, go along يضم yadumm
joke نكتة nukta
journalist صحافي sahaafii
journey سفر safar
jug, pitcher إبريق 'ibriiq
juice عصير 'asiir
July تموز tammuuz
jump, to يقفز yaqfiz
June حزيران huzayraan
jungle غابة ghaaba
just, only فقط faqat
just, fair منصف munsif
just now ألآن al'aan

K

keep, to يحفظ yahfaz
key (to room) مفتاح miftaah
key (computer) مفتاح miftaah
keyboard (of computer) لوحة المفاتيح lawhat al-mafaatiih
kidney كلية kilya
kidney beans الفاصوليا al-faasuulyia
kill, murder يقتل yaqtul
kilogram كيلو kiilu
kilometre كيلومتر kilumitir
kind, good (of persons) طيب tayyib
kind, type نوع naw'
king ملك malik
kiss قبلة qubla
kiss, to يقبل yuqabbil
kitchen مطبخ matbakh
kiwi fruit الكيوي al-kiiwii
knee ركبة rukba
knife سكين sikkiin
knock, to يدق yaduqq
know, to يعرف ya'rif
know, be acquainted with يعرف ya'rif
knowledge معرفة ma'rifa
Korea, North كوريا الشمالية kuriya ash-shamaaliya
Korea, South كوريا الجنوبية kuriya al-januubiya
Korean كوري kuurii

L

lacking ناقص naaqis
ladder سلم sullam
ladle, dipper مغرفة mighrafa
lady سيدة sayyida
lake بحيرة buhayra
lamb, mutton خروف kharuuf
lamp مصباح misbaah
land أرض 'ard
land, to (plane) يهبط yahbit
lane (of a highway) خط khatt
lane (alley) ممر mamar
language لغة lugha
Laos لاووس laawuus
Laotian لاووسي laawuusii
large كبير kabiir
last آخر 'aakhir
last night البارحة al-baariha
last week الأسبوع الماضي al-'usbuu' al-maadii
last year السنة الماضية as-sana al-maadiya
late متأخر muta'akhkhir
late at night متأخر muta'akhkhir
later لاحقا laahiqan
laugh, to يضحك yadhak
laugh at, to يضحق على yadhak 'ala

laws, legislation قوانين qawaaniin
lawyer محامي muhaamii
layer طبقة tabaqa
lay the table يمد الطاولة yamudd at-tawila
lazy كسول kasuul
lead (to be a leader) يحكم yahkum
lead (to guide someone somewhere) يقود yaquud
leader حاكم haakim
leaf ورقة نبات waraqat nabaat
leak, to يتسرب yatasarrab
learn, to يتعلم yata'allam
least (smallest amount) أقل 'aqal
least: at least على الأقل 'ala al-'aqal
leather جلد jild
leave, depart يترك yatruk
leave behind by accident ينسى yansaa
leave behind on purpose يترك yatruk
leave behind for safekeeping يحفظ yahfaz
lecture محاضرة muhaadara
lecturer (at university) محاضر muhaadir
left, remaining متبقي mutabaqqii
left-hand side يسار yasaar
leg رجل rijl
legal قانوني qaanuunii
legend أسطورة ustuura
lemon, citrus حامض haamid
lemongrass الأعشقب الليمونية al-a'shaab al-laymuuniya
lend, to يعير yu'iir
length طول tuul
less (smaller amount) أقل 'aqal
less, minus أقل 'aqal
lessen, reduce يخفف yukhaffif
lesson درس dars
let, allow يسمح yasmah
let's (suggestion) لـ li...
let someone know, to يخبر yukhbir
letter رسالة risaala
level (even, flat) يسوي yusawwi
level (height) مستوى الإرتفاع mustawaa al-'irtifaa'
level (standard) مستوى mustawaa
library مكتبة maktaba
licence (for driving) ترخيص tarkhiis
licence, permit اذن 'idhin
lick, to يلحس yalhas
lid غطاء ghitaa'
lie, tell a falsehood يكذب yakdhib
lie down, to يستلقي yastalqii
life حياة hayaat
lifetime عمر 'umr
lift, elevator مصعد mis'ad
lift (ride in car) ينقل yanqul
lift, raise يرفع yarfa'
light (not heavy) خفيف khafiif
light (bright) ساطع saati'
light (lamp) ضوء daw'
lighter قداحة qaddaaha
lightning برق barq
like, as مثل mithil
like, be pleased by يحب yuhibb
likewise أيضا 'aydan
lime, citrus حامض haamid
line (mark) خط khatt
line (queue) صف saff
line up, to يقف بالصف yaqif bis-saff

L

lips شفاه shifaah
liquor, alcohol كحول kuhuul
list لائحة laa'iha
listen اصغاء 'isghaa'
listen to يسمع yasma'
literature أدب 'adab
little (not much) قليل qaliil
little (small) صغير saghiir
live (be alive) يعيش ya'iish
live (stay in a place) يسكن yaskun
liver كبد kabid
load حمل himl
load up, to يحمل yuhammil
located, to be واقع waaqi'
lock قفل qifl
lock, to يقفل yaqfil
locked مقفول maqfuul
lodge, small hotel فندق funduq
lonely وحيد wahiid
long (time) طويل tawiil
long (length) طول tuul
look! أنظر 'unzur
look at, see ينظر yanzur
look, seem, appear يظهر yazhar
look after يهتم بـ yahtam bi
look for يفتش yufattish
look like يشبه yushbih
look out! انتبه 'intabih
look up (find in book) يبحث yabhath
loose (wobbly) لين layyin
loose (not in packet) محلول mahluul
lose, be defeated يخسر yakhsir
lose, mislay يضيع yudayyi'
lose money, to يخسر yakhsir
lost (missing) مفقود mafquud
lost (can't find way) ضائع daa'i'
lost property ضائع daa'i'
lots of الكثير من al-kathiir min
lottery اليانصيب al-yaanasiib
loud صاخب saakhib
love حب hubb
love, to يحب yuhibb
lovely محبب muhabbab
low منخفض munkhafid
luck حظ hazz
lucky محظوظ mahzuuz
luggage أمتعة 'amti'a
lunch, midday meal غداء ghadhaa'
lunch, to eat يتناول الغداء yatanaawal al-ghadhaa'
lungs رئة ri'a
luxurious رفاهي rafaahii
lychee لايتشي laaytchii

M

machine آلة 'aala
machinery آلات 'aalaat
madam (term of address) سيدة sayyida
magazine مجلة majalla
mah jong ماجونغ maajungh
mail, post بريد bariid
mail, to يرسل yursil
main, most important أهم 'ahamm
mainly جدا jiddan
major (important) أهم 'ahamm
make, to يصنع yasna'
make do يفعل yaf'al
make up, invent يخترع yakhtari'
Malaysia ماليزيا maaliizyaa
Malaysian ماليزي maaliizi
male ذكر dhakar
man رجل rajul
manage, succeed ينجح yanjah
manager مدير mudiir

mango المنجا al-manjaa
manufacture, to يصنع yasna'
many, much كثير kathiir
map خريطة khariita
March آذار 'aadhaar
market سوق suuq
married متزوج mutazawwij
marry, get married يتزوج yatazawwaj
mask قناع qinaa'
massage, to يدلك yudallik
mat حصير hasiir
match, game مباراة mubaaraat
matches فتيل fatiil
material, ingredient مواد mawaad
matter, issue أمر 'amr
matter, it doesn't لا يهم laa yahumm
mattress فراش firaash
May أيار 'ayyar
may يستطيع yastatii'
maybe ربما rubbama
meal وجبة wajba
mean (cruel) قاس qaasin
mean, to (intend) يقصد yaqsid
mean, to (word) يعني ya'nii
meaning معنى ma'na
meanwhile بينما baynamaa
measure, to يقيس yaqiis
measurement قياس qiyaas
measure out يناسب yunaasib
meat لحم lahm
meatball الكرة اللحمية al-kura al-lahmiyya
medical طبي tibbii
medicine طب tibb
meet, to يلتقي yaltaqii
meeting لقاء liqaa'
melon بطيخ battiikh
member عضو 'udwu
memories ذكريات dhikrayaat
mend, to يصلح yuslih
menstruate, to تحيض tuhiid
mention, to يذكر yadhkur
menu قائمة الطعام qaa'imat at-ta'aam
merely فحسب fahasb
mess, in a فوضى fawdaa
message رسالة risaala
metal معدن ma'dan
method طريقة tariiqa
midday ظهر zuhr
middle, centre وسط wasat
middle: be in the middle of doing وسط wasat
midnight منتصف الليل muntasaf al-layl
mild (not spicy) غير حاد ghayr haadd
mild (not severe) معتدل mu'tadil
milk حليب haliib
million مليون milyuun
mind, brain عقل 'aql
mind, to be displeased يعارض yu'aarid
minibus حفلة صغيرة haafila saghiira
minor (not important) ثانوي، بسيط thaanawii; basiit
minus ناقص naaqis
minute دقيقة daqiiqa
mirror مرآة mir'aat
misfortune محنة mihna
miss, to (bus, flight) يفوت yufawwit
miss, to (loved one) يشتاق yashtaaq
missing (absent) غائب ghaa'ib
missing (lost person) مفقود mafquud
mist غشاوة ghashaawa
mistake غلطة ghalta
mistaken مخطئ mukhti'

M

ENGLISH–ARABIC

misunderstanding سوء تفاهم suu' tafaahum
mix, to يخلط yakhlut
mixed خليط khaliit
mobile phone الهاتف الجوال al-haatif al-jawwaal
modern عصري 'asrii
modest, simple متواضع mutawaadi'
moment (instant) لحظة lahza
moment (in a moment, just a moment) لحظة lahza
Monday الاثنين al-'ithnayn
money مال maal
monitor (of computer) شاشة shaasha
monkey قرد qird
month شهر shahr
monument أثر 'athar
moon قمر qamar
more (comparative) اكثر akthar
more of (things) اكثر akthar
more or less تقريبا taqriiban
morning صباح sabaah
mosque جامع jaami'
mosquito ذبابة dhubaaba
most (superlative) الأكثر al-akthar
most (the most of) الأكثر al-akthar
mostly في الأغلب fi al-aghlab
moth فراشة faraasha
mother أم 'umm
mother-in-law الحماة al-hamaa
motor, engine محرك muharrik
motorcycle دراجة darraja
motor vehicle سيارة sayyara
mountain جبل jabal
mouse (animal) فأر fa'r
mouse (computer) فأرة الكمبيوتر fa'ratu l-kambyuutar
moustache شارب shaarib
mouth فم famm
move, to يتحرك yataharrak
move from one place to another يتنقل yatanaqqal
movement, motion حركة haraka
movie فيلم film
movie house قاعة السينما qaa'at as-siinimaa
much, many كثير kathiir
muscle عضل 'adal
mushroom فطر fitr
music موسيقى muusiiqaa
Muslim مسلم muslim
must يجب yajib
my, mine لي lii
myth أسطورة 'ustuura

N

nail (finger, toe) ظفر zifr
nail (spike) مسمار mismaar
naked عار aarin
name اسم 'ism
narrow ضيق dayyiq
nation, country دولة dawla
national دولي duwali
nationality جنسية jinsiyya
natural طبيعي tabii'ii
nature الطبيعة at-tabii'a
naughty سيء السلوك sayi' as-suluuk
nearby قريب qariib
nearly تقريبا taqriiban
neat, orderly قديم qadiim
necessary مهم muhim
neck عنق 'unuq
necklace عقد 'iqd
necktie ربطة العنق rabtat al-'unq
need حاجة haaja
need, to يحتاج yahtaaj
needle إبرة 'ibra

neighbour جار jaar
neither لا أحد laa 'ahad
neither...nor لا هذا و لا ذلك laa haadha wa laa dhaalik
nephew ابن الأخ ibn al-'akh
nest عش 'ush
net شبكة shabaka
network شبكة shabaka
never أبدا 'abadan
never mind! لا يهم laa yahumm
nevertheless و مع ذلك wa ma'a dhaalika
new جديد jadiid
news أخبار 'akhbaar
newspaper جريدة jariida
New Zealand نيو زلندا niyu ziilandaa
next (in line, sequence) الموالي al-muwaalii
next to إلى جانب 'ila jaanib
next week الأسبوع القادم al-usbuu' al-qaadim
next year السنة القادمة as-sana al-qaadima
nice حسن hasan
niece ابنة الأخ 'ibnat al-'akh
night ليل layl
nightclothes ثياب النوم thiyaab an-nawm
nightdress البيجاما al-biijaama
nightly ليلي layliy
nine تسعة tis'a
nineteen تسعة عشر tis'ata 'ashar
ninety تسعين tis'iin
no, not (with nouns and adjectives) ليس laysa
no, not (with verbs) لا laa
nobody لا أحد laa 'ahad
noise ضجيج dajiij
noisy ضاج daajj
nonsense هراء huraa'
noodles العصائبية al-'asaa'ibiyya
noon ظهر zuhr
nor و لا wa laa
normal طبيعي tabii'ii
normally عادة 'aadatan
north شمال shamaal
north-east شمال شرق shamaal sharq
north-west شمال غرب shamaal gharb
nose أنف 'anf
nostril ثقب الأنف thuqb al-anf
not لا laa
not only...but also لا و لكن laa wa laakin
not yet ليس بعد laysa ba'du
note (written) ملاحظة mulaahaza
note (currency) ورقة نقدية waraqa naqdiyya
notebook دفتر daftar
note down, to يكتب yaktub
nothing لا شيء laa shay'
notice ملاحظة mulaahaza
notice, to يلاحظ yulaahiz
novel رواية riwaaya
November تشرين الثاني tishriin ath-thaani
now الان al-'aan
nowadays في هذا العصر fii haadha l-'asr
nowhere و لا مكن wa laa makaan
nude عار 'aarin
numb مخدر mukhaddar
number عدد 'adad
nylon نيلون naylun

O

o'clock تمام الساعة tamaam as-saa'a
obedient مطيع mutii'

ENGLISH–ARABIC

O

obey, to يطيع yutii'

object, thing شيء <u>sh</u>ay'

object, to protest يعترض ya'tari<u>d</u>

occasionally أحيانا 'a<u>h</u>yaanan

occupation مهنة mihna

ocean محيط mu<u>h</u>iit

October تشرين الأول ti<u>sh</u>riin al-'awwal

odour, bad smell رائحة كريهة raa'i<u>h</u>a kariiha

of, from من min

of course طبعا <u>t</u>ab'an

off (gone bad) فاسد faasid

off (turned off) منطفئ munt̩afi'

off: to turn something off يطفئ yut̩fi'

offend يهين yuhiin

offer, suggest يقترح yaqtari<u>h</u>

offering عرض 'ar<u>d</u>

office مكتب maktab

official, formal رسمي rasmii

officials (government) حكومة <u>h</u>ukuuma

often غالبا <u>gh</u>aaliban

oil زيت zayt

okay حسنا <u>h</u>asanan

old (of persons) عجوز 'ajuuz

old (of things) قديم qadiim

olden times, in في الماضي fii l-maa<u>d</u>ii

older brother or sister الأخ أو الأخت الأكبر al-'a<u>kh</u> 'aw al-'u<u>kh</u>t al-'akbar

on, at على 'alaa

on (of dates) في fii

on (turned on) مشغل mu<u>sh</u>a<u>gh</u>al

on: to turn something on يشغل yu<u>sh</u>a<u>gh</u>il

on board على ظهر 'alaa <u>z</u>ahr

on fire يحترق ya<u>h</u>tariq

on foot على الأقدام 'alaa al-'aqdaam

on the way على الطريق 'alaa t̩-t̩ariiq

on the whole إجمالا ijmaalan

on time في الوقت المحدد fii l-waqt al-mu<u>h</u>addad

once مرة marratan

one واحد waa<u>h</u>id

one-way ticket تذكرة إتجاة واحد ta<u>dh</u>karat ittijaah waa<u>h</u>id

one who, the one which الذي alla<u>dh</u>ii

onion بصل ba<u>s</u>al

only فقط faqat̩

open مفتوح maftuu<u>h</u>

open, to يفتح yafta<u>h</u>

opinion رأي ra'i

opponent الخصم al-<u>kh</u>asim

opportunity فرصة fur<u>s</u>a

oppose, to يعارض yu'aari<u>d</u>

opposed, in opposition بالمقارنة bil-muqaarana

opposite (facing) مواجه muwaajih

opposite (contrary) ضد <u>d</u>idd

optional اختياري 'i<u>kh</u>tiyaari

or أو 'aw

orange, citrus ليمون laymuun

orange (colour) ليموني laymuuni

order (command) أمر 'amr

order (placed for food, goods) طلب t̩alab

order, sequence ترتيب tartiib

order, to command يأمر ya'mur

order something, to يطلب yat̩lub

orderly, organised منظم muna<u>zz</u>am

organise, arrange ينظم yuna<u>zz</u>im

origin أصل 'a<u>s</u>l
original أصلى 'a<u>s</u>lii
originate, come from يبدأ yabda'
ornament زينة ziina
other غير <u>gh</u>ayr
ought to يجب yajib
our (excludes the one addressed) لنا جميعا lanaa jamii'an
our (includes the one addressed) لنا lanaa
out إلى الخارج 'ila al-<u>kh</u>aarij
outside خارج <u>kh</u>aarij
outside of خارج <u>kh</u>arija
oval (shape) بيضوي bay<u>d</u>awii
oven فرن furn
over, finished انتهى 'intaha
over: to turn over إلى الجانب الآخر 'ila al-jaanib al-'aa<u>kh</u>ar
overcast, cloudy غائم <u>gh</u>aa'im
overcome, to يتغلب على yata<u>gh</u>allab 'alaa
overseas خارجي <u>kh</u>aarijii
over there هناك hunaak
overturned مقلوب maqluub
owe, to يدين yadiin
own, to يملك yamlik
own, personal شخصي <u>sh</u>a<u>kh</u>sii
own, on one's بنفسه binafsihi
oyster المحارة al-ma<u>h</u>aara

P

pack, to يحزم ya<u>h</u>zim
package رزمة ruzma
page صفحة <u>s</u>af<u>h</u>a
paid مدفوع madfuu'
pain ألم 'alam
painful مؤلم mu'lim
paint دهان dihaan
paint, to (a painting) يرسم yarsum

paint, to (house, furniture) يدهن yadhan
painting لوحة law<u>h</u>a
pair of, a جوز jawz
pajamas ثياب النوم <u>th</u>iyaab an-nawm
palace (Balinese) بلاط balaa<u>t</u>
palace (Javanese) قصر qa<u>s</u>r
pan مقلاة miqlaat
panorama البانوراما al-baanuuraamaa
panties سروال تحتي sirwaal ta<u>h</u>tii
pants بنطلون bantalun
papaya البابايا al-babaayaa
paper ورق waraq
parcel طرد <u>t</u>ard
pardon me? what did you say? عفوا 'afwan
parents أهل 'ahl
park حديقة <u>h</u>adiiqa
park, to (car) يوقف السيارة yuuqif as-sayyaara
part (not whole) جزء juz'
part (of machine) قطعة qi<u>t</u>'a
participate, to يشارك yu<u>sh</u>aarik
particularly, especially خصوصا <u>kh</u>u<u>s</u>uu<u>s</u>an
partly جزئيا juz'iyyan
partner (in business) شريك <u>sh</u>ariik
partner (spouse) زوج zawj
party (event) حفل <u>h</u>afl
party (political) حزب <u>h</u>izb
pass, go past يعبر ya'bur
pass, to (exam) ينجح yanja<u>h</u>
passenger راكب raakib
passionfruit غلال الباشين <u>gh</u>ilaal al-baa<u>sh</u>in
passport سفر جواز jawaaz safar
past: go past يمر yamurr
past, former سابق saabiq
pastime تسلية tasliya

patient (calm) صابر saabir
patient (doctor's) مريض mariid
pattern, design نموذج namuudhaj
patterned منمط munammat
pay, to يدفع yadfa'
pay attention ينتبه yantabih
payment دفعة duf'a
peace أمن 'amn
peaceful مسلام musaalim
peak, summit قمة qimma
peanut فول سوداني fuul suudaanii
pearl لؤلؤ lu'lu'
peas البازلا al-baazilla
peel, to يقشر yuqashshir
pen قلم qalam
pencil قلم رصاص qalam rasaas
penis قضيب qadiib
people الناس an-naas
pepper, black بهار bahaar
pepper, chilli فلفل fulful
percent بالمئة bilmi'a
percentage نسبة مئوية nisba mi'awiyya
performance تأدية ta'diya
perfume عطر 'itr
perhaps, maybe ربما rubbama
perhaps, probably لعل la'alla
period (end of a sentence) نقطة nuqta
period (of time) فترة fitra
period (menstrual) الدور الشهرية addawra ash-shariya
permanent دائم daa'im
permit, licence رخصة rukhsa
permit, to allow يرخص yurakhkhis
person شخص shakhs
personality شخصية shakhsiyya
perspire, to يعرق ya'raq
pet animal حيوان أليف hayawaan 'aliif
petrol بنزين banziin
petrol station محطة بنزين mahattat banziin
pharmacy, drugstore صيدلية saydaliyya
Philippines الفيليبين al-filippiin
photocopy نسخة nuskha
photocopy, to ينسخ yansakh
photograph صورة suura
photograph, to يصور yusawwir
pick, choose يختار yakhtaar
pick up, to (someone) يقل yuqill
pick up, lift (something) يحمل yahmil
pickpocket النشال al-nashshaal
pickpocket, to ينشل yanshul
picture صورة suura
piece, portion, section جزء juz'
piece, item قطعة qit'a
pierce, penetrate يثقب yathqub
pig خنزير khanziir
pills حبوب hubuub
pillow وسادة wisaada
pineapple أناناس 'anaanaas
pink زهري zahrii
pitcher, jug إبريق 'ibriiq
pity: what a pity! خسارة khasaara
place مكان makaan
place, put يضع yada'
plain (not fancy) بسيط basiit
plain (level ground) أرضي 'ardii
plan خطة khutta
plan, to يخطط yukhattit
plane طائرة taa'ira
plant نبتة nabta
plant, to يزرع yazra'

plastic بلاستيك blaastiik
plate طبق tabaq
play, to يلعب yal'ab
play around يتلاعب yatalaa'ab
plead, to يدافع yudaafi'
pleasant لطيف latiif
please (go ahead) تفضل tafaddal
please (request for help) أرجو 'arju
please (request for something) من فضلك min fadlik
pleased سعيد sa'iid
plug (bath) سدة sudda
plug (electric) المأخذ al-ma'khadh
plum خوخ khawkh
plus زائد zaa'id
pocket جيب jayb
point (in time) فترة fitra
point, dot نقطة nuqta
point out يدل yadull
poison سم summ
poisonous سام saam
police شرطة shurta
police officer ضابط شرطة daabit shurta
polish, to يلمع yulammi'
politics سياسة siyaasa
polite مهذب muhadhdhab
poor فقير faqiir
popular معروف ma'ruuf
population عدد السكان 'adad as-sukkaan
pork لحم خنزير lahm khanziir
port مرفئ marfa'
portion, serve حصة hissa
possess, to يملك yamlik
possessions ممتلكات mumtalakaat
possible ممكن mumkin
possibly ربما rubbamaa
post, column عمود 'amuud
post, mail بريد bariid
postcard بطاقة بريدية bitaaqa bariidiyya
post office البريد al-bariid
postpone, to يؤجل yu'ajjil
postponed, delayed مؤجل mu'ajjal
pot قدر qidr
potato بطاطا bataataa
poultry دواجن dawaajin
pour, to يصب yasubb
power قوة quwwa
powerful قوي qawii
practice تدريب tadriib
practice, to يتدرب yatadarrab
praise إطراء 'itraa'
praise, to يطري yutrii
prawn القريدس al-quraydis
pray, to يصلي yusallii
prayer صلاة salaat
prefer, to يفضل yufaddil
pregnant حامل haamil
prepare, make ready يحضر yuhaddir
prepared, ready حاضر haadir
prescription وصفة طبية wasfa tibbiyya
present (here) هنا huna
present (gift) هدية hadiyya
present, to يقدم yuqaddim
present moment, at the في الوقت الحاضر fii al-waqt al-haadir
presently, nowadays ألآن al-'aan
president رئيس ra'iis
press, journalism صحافة sahaafa
press, to يضغط yadghat
pressure ضغط daghit
pretend, to يدعي yadda'ii

ENGLISH–ARABIC

P

ENGLISH–ARABIC

pretty (of places, things) خلاب khallab
pretty (of women) جميل jamiil
pretty, very كثير kathiir
prevent, to يتحاشى yatahaashaa
price سعر si'r
pride كبرياء kibriyaa'
priest كاهن kaahin
prime minister رئيس الوزراء ra'iis al-wuzaraa'
print, to يطبع yatba'
prison سجن sijn
private شخصي shakhsii
probably ربما rubbama
problem مشكلة mushkila
produce, to يصنع yasna'
profession مهنة mihna
profit ربح ribh
program, schedule برنامج barnaamaj
promise, to يعد ya'id
pronounce, to يلفظ yalfaz
proof دليل daliil
property ملكية milkiyya
protest, to يحتج yahtajj
proud فخور fakhuur
prove, to يثبت yuthbit
public عام 'aam
publish, to ينشر yanshur
pull, to يسحب yashab
pump مضخة midakhkha
punctual دقيق daqiiq
pupil تلميذ tilmiidh
pure نقي naqii
purple أرجواني 'urjuwaanii
purpose هدف hadaf
purse (for money) محفظة mihfaza
push, to يدفع yadfa'
put, place يضع yada'
put off, delay يؤجل yu'ajjil
put on (clothes) يرتدي yartadii
puzzled مرتبك murtabik
pyjamas لباس النوم libaas an-nawm

Q

qualification الشهادات ash-shahaadaat
quarter ربع rub'
queen ملكة malika
question سؤال su'aal
queue, line دور dawr
queue, to line up يقف بالدور yaqif bid-dawr
quick سريع sarii'
quickly بسرعة bisur'a
quiet هادئ haadi'
quite (fairly) فعلا fi'lan
quite (very) كثير kathiir

R

raadiyu راديو raadiyu
rail: by rail بالقطار bi-lqitaar
railroad, railway سكك حديدية sikak hadiidiyya
rain مطر matar
rain, to تمطر tumtir
raise, lift يرفع yarfa'
raise, to (children) يربي yurabbii
rank, station in life الرتبة ar-rutba
ranking ترتيب tartiib
rare (scarce) نادر naadir
rare (uncooked) نيئ nay'
rarely, seldom نادرا naadiran
rat فأر fa'r
rate, tariff ضريبة dariiba
rate of exchange (for foreign currency) سعر si'r
rather, fairly بالأحرى bil'ahra
rather than أفضل من afdal min

raw, uncooked, rare غير ناضج ghayr naadij
reach, get to يصل yasil
react to يتفاعل yatafaa'al
reaction, response رد radd
read, to يقرأ yaqra'
ready جاهز jaahiz
ready, to get يجهز yajhaz
ready, to make يجهز yujahhiz
realise, be aware of يدرك yudrik
really (in fact) حقا haqqan
really (very) كثير kathiir
really? حقا haqqan
rear, tail مؤخرة mu'akhkhara
reason سبب sabab
reasonable (sensible) عاقل 'aaqil
reasonable (price) معقول ma'quul
receipt فاتورة faatuura
receive, to يستلم yastalim
recipe وصفة wasfa
recognise, to يتعرف yata'arraf
recommend, to يقترح yaqtarih
recovered, cured شاف shaafin
rectangle مستطيل mustatiil
red أحمر 'ahmar
reduce, to يخفف yukhaffif
reduction تخفيف takhfiif
reflect, to يعكس ya'kis
refrigerator ثلاجة thallaaja
refusal رفض rafd
refuse, to يرفض yarfud
regarding بالنسبة إلى bin-nisba ilaa
region منطقة mintaqa
register, to يسجل yusajjil
registered post بريد مسجل bariid musajjal
regret, to يندم yandam
regrettably للأسف lil'asaf
regular, normal عادي 'aadii
relatives, family أقارب 'aqaarib
relax, to يرتاح yartaah
release, to يطلق سراح yutliq saraah
religion ديانة diyaana
remainder, leftover بقية baqiyya
remains (historical) اثار 'aathaar
remember, to يتذكر yatadhakkar
remind, to يذكر yudhakkir
rent, to يؤجر yu'ajjir
rent out, to يستأجر yasta'jir
repair, to يصلح yuslih
repeat, to يعيد yu'iid
replace, to يغير yughayyir
reply, response جواب jawaab
reply, to (in writing or deeds) يرد yarudd
reply, to (in speech) يرد yarudd
report تقرير taqriir
report, to يخبر yukhbir
reporter مخبر mukhbir
request, to (formally) يطلب yatlub
request, to (informally) يطلب yatlub
rescue, to ينقذ yunqidh
research بحث bahth
research, to يبحث yabhath
resemble يشبه yushbih
reservation حجز hajz
reserve (for animals) إحتياطي ihtiyaatiy
reserve, to (ask for in advance) يحجز yahjiz
resident, inhabitant مقيم muqiim
resolve, to (a problem) يحل yahill
respect احترام 'ihtiraam
respect, to يحترم yahtarim

respond, react يرد ، الفعل yarudd; al-fi'l
response, reaction رد radd
responsibility مسؤولية mas'uuliyya
responsible, to be مسؤول mas'uul
rest, remainder بقية baqiyya
rest, to relax يرتاح yartaah
restaurant مطعم mat'am
restrain, to يكبح yakbah
restroom حجرة الراحة hujrat ar-raaha
result نتيجة natiija
resulting from, as a result نتيجة لـ natiijatan li
retired متقاعد mutaqaa'id
return, go back يرجع yarji'
return, give back يعيد yu'iid
return home, to يعود ya'uud
return ticket تذكرة العودة tadhkarat al-'awda
reveal, to (make visible) يكشف yakshif
reveal, to (make known) يعلن yu'lin
reverse, to back up يرجع yarji'
reversed, backwards عكسي 'aksii
ribbon شريط shariit
rice (cooked) أرز 'aruzz
rice (uncooked grains) أرز 'aruzz
rice (plant) نبتة الأرز nabtat al-'aruzz
rice fields حقول الأرز huquul al-'aruzz
rich غني ghanii
rid: get rid of يتخلص من yatakhallas min
ride (in car) رحلة rihla
ride, to (animal) يركب yarkab
ride, to (transport) يركب yarkab
right, correct صحيح sahiih
right-hand side يمين yamiin
right now الان al-'aan
rights حقوق huquuq
ring (jewellery) خاتم khaatam
ring, to (on the telephone) يتصل yattasil
ring, to (bell) يرن yarinn
ripe ناضج naadij
rise, ascend يصعد yas'ad
rise, increase يرتفع yartafi'
rival منافس munaafis
river نهر nahir
road طريق tariiq
roast, grill لحم مشوي lahm mashwii
roasted, grilled, toasted مشوي mashwii
rock صخرة sakhra
role دور dawr
roof سطح satih
room (in house) غرفة ghurfa
room (in hotel) غرفة ghurfa
room, space مسافة masaafa
root (of plant) جذر jidhir
rope حبل habl
rotten نتن natin
rough قاس qaasin
roughly, approximately تقريبا taqriiban
round (shape) مدور mudawwar
round, around حول hawla
rubber مطاط mattaat
rude فظ fazz
rules قوانين qawaaniin
run, to يركض yarkud
run away يهرب yahrab

S

sacred مقدس muqadaas

sacrifice تضحية tad-hiya
sacrifice, to يضحي yudahhi
sad حزين haziin
safe امن 'aamin
sail, to يبحر yubhir
salary راتب raatib
sale, for للبيع lil-bay'
sale (reduced prices) خصم khasm
sales assistant بائع baa'i'
salt ملح milh
salty مالح maalih
same مطابق mutaabiq
sample عينة 'ayyina
sand تراب turaab
sandals صندل sandal
satisfied مكتفي muktafii
satisfy, to يكفي yakfii
Saturday السبت as-sabt
sauce صلصة salsa
sauce (chilli) صلصة الفلفل salsat al-fulful
save, keep يحفظ yahfaz
say, to يقول yaquul
say hello يسلم yusallim
say goodbye يودع yuwaddi'
say sorry يعتذر ya'tadhir
say thankyou يشكر yashkur
scales درجات darajaat
scarce نادر naadir
scared خائف khaa'if
scenery مشهد mashhad
schedule برنامج barnaamaj
school مدرسة madrasa
schoolchild طالب taalib
science علم 'ilm
scissors مقص miqas
Scotland سكوتلندا skutlandaa
Scottish, Scots سكوتلندي skutlandii
screen (of computer) شاشة shaasha
scrub, to يفرك yafruk
sculpt, to ينحت yanhat
sculpture تمثال timthaal
sea بحر bahr
seafood أكل بحري 'akl bahrii
search for, to يبحث yabhath
season فصل fasl
seat مقعد maq'ad
second ثانية thaaniya
secret سر sirr
secret, to keep a يحفظ سر yahfaz sirr
secretary سكرتير sikritiir
secure, safe امن 'aamin
see, to يرى yaraa
seed بذرة badhra
seek, to يبحث yabhath
seem, to يبدو yabduu
see you later! الى اللقاء 'ila al-liqaa'
seldom نادرا naadiran
select, to يختار yakhtaar
self نفسي nafsii
sell, to يبيع yabii'
send, to يرسل yursil
sensible عاقل 'aaqil
sentence جملة jumla
separate منفصل munfasil
separate, to يفصل yafsil
September أيلول 'ayluul
sequence, order تدرج tadarruj
serious (not funny) جدي jiddii
serious (severe) خطر khatir
servant خادم khaadim
serve, to يخدم yakhdim
service خدمة khidma
sesame oil زيت السمسم zayt as-simsim
sesame seeds حب السمسم habb as-simsim
set طقم taqim
seven سبعة sab'a

S

seventeen سبعة عشر sab'ata 'ashar
seventy سبعين sab'iin
several عدة 'iddat
severe قاس qaasin
sew, to يخيط yukhayyit
sex, gender جنس jins
sex, sexual activity جنس jins
shack كوخ kuukh
shade ظل zill
shadow خيال khayaal
shadow play خيال الظل khayaal az-zill
shake, to يرتج yartajj
shake something, to يمزج yamzuj
shall, will سوف sawfa
shallow سطحي sat-hii
shame, disgrace عار 'aar
shame: what a shame! يا للأسف yaa la-l'asaf
shampoo شامبو shaambuu
shape شكل shakl
shape, to form يشكل yushakkil
shark قرش qirsh
sharp حاد haad
shave, to يحلق yahliq
she, her هي hiya
sheet (of paper) ورقة waraqa
sheet (for bed) غطاء ghitaa'
sheep ماعز maa'iz
Shinto ديانة شنتو اليابانية diyaanat shintu al-yaabaaniyya
shiny لامع laami'
ship باخرة baakhira
shirt قميص qamiis
shit براز buraaz
shiver, to يرتجف yartajif
shoes حذاء hidhaa'
shoot, to يطلق النار yutliq an-naar
shop, store محل mahall
shop, go shopping يتسوق yatasawwaq
shopkeeper صاحب المحل saahib al-mahall
short (concise) مختصر mukhtasar
short (not tall) قصير qasiir
shorts (short trousers) تبان tubbaan
shorts (underpants) ملابس داخلية malaabis daakhiliyya
short time, a moment لحظة lahza
shoulder كتف katif
shout, to يصرخ yasrukh
show (broadcast) برنامج barnaamaj
show (live performance) حفل hafl
show, to يظهر yuzhir
shower (for washing) دش dush
shower (of rain) وابل من المطر waabil mina l-matar
shower, to take a يغتسل yaghtasil
shrimp, prawn قريدس quraydis
shut مغلق mughlaq
shut, to يغلق yughliq
sibling أخ 'akh
sick, ill مريض mariid
sick to be (vomit) يمرض yamrad
side جهة jiha
sightseeing التنزه at-tanazzuh
sign, symbol اشارة 'ishaara
sign, to يوقع yuwaqqi'
signature توقيع tawqii'
signboard لافتة laafita
silent هادئ haadi'
silk حرير hariir
silver فضة fidda

similar متشابه mutashaabih
simple (easy) بسيط basiit
simple (uncomplicated, modest) متواضع mutawaadi'
since منذ mundhu
sing, to يغني yughanni
Singapore سنغفورة sanghafuura
single (not married) أعزب a'zab
single (only one) منفرد munfarid
sir (term of address) سيد sayyid
sister أخت 'ukht
sister-in-law زوجة الأخ zawjatu l-'akh
sit, to يجلس yajlis
sit down, to يجلس yajlis
situated, to be قائم qaa'im
situation, how things are حالة haala
six ستة sitta
sixteen ستة عشر sittata 'ashar
sixty ستين sittiin
size قياس qiyaas
skewer سفود saffuud
skilful بارع baari'
skin بشرة bashara
skirt تنورة tannuura
sky سماء samaa'
sleep, to ينام yanaam
sleepy نعسان na'saan
slender نحيل nahiil
slight خفيف khafiif
slightly قليلا qaliilan
slim نحيل nahiil
slip (petticoat, underskirt) يضع yada'
slippers شبشب shibshib
slope منحدر munhadar
slow بطيء batii'
slowly ببطء bi-but'
small صغير saghiir
smart ذكي dhakii
smell, bad odour رائحة كريهة raa'iha kariiha
smell, to يشم yashumm
smile, to يبتسم yabtasim
smoke دخان dukhaan
smoke, to (tobacco) يدخن yudakhkhin
smooth (to go smoothly) بلطف bilutf
smooth (of surfaces) مالس maalis
smuggle, to يهرب yuharrib
snake أفعى 'af'a
sneeze عطسة 'atsa
sneeze, to يعطس ya'tis
snow ثلج thalj
snow, to تثلج tuthlij
snowpeas البازلاء al-baazilla'
so, therefore لذلك lidhaalika
soak, to يبلل yuballil
soap صابون saabuun
soccer كرة القدم kurat al-qadam
socket (electric) مقبس maqbis
socks جوارب jawaarib
sofa, couch أريكة 'ariika
soft ناعم naa'im
soft drink شراب sharaab
sold مباع mubaa'
soldier جندي jundii
sold out نافذ naafidh
sole, only وحيد wahiid
solid صلب salb
solve, to (a problem) يحل yahill
some بعض ba'd
somebody, someone شخص ما shakhs maa
something شيء shay'
sometimes أحيانا 'ahyaanan
somewhere مكان ما makaan maa

son ابن 'ibn
son-in-law صهر sihr
song أغنية 'ughniya
soon قريبا qariiban
sore, painful مؤلم mu'lim
sorrow حزن huzn
sorry, to feel regretful اسف 'aasif
sorry! عفوا 'afwan
sort, type نوع naw'
sort out, deal with يحل yahill
so that حتى hattaa
sound, noise صوت sawt
soup (clear) ضباب dabaab
soup (spicy stew) حساء hisaa'
sour حامض haamid
source منبع manba'
south جنوب januub
south-east جنوب شرق januub sharq
south-west جنوب غرب januub gharb
souvenir تذكار tadhkaar
so very كثير kathiir
soy sauce (salty) صلصة الصويا (المالحة) salsat as-suuyaa (al-maaliha)
soy sauce (sweet) صلصة الصويا (الحلوة) salsat as-suuyaa (al-hulwa)
space مسافة masaafa
spacious واسع waasi'
speak, to يتكلم yatakallam
special مميز mumayyaz
spectacles نظارات nazzaaraat
speech خطاب khitaab
speech, to make a يلقي خطاب yulqii khitaab
speed سرعة sur'a
spell, to يتهجى yatahajjaa
spend, to يصرف yasrif
spices توابل tawaabil
spicy كثير التوابل kathiir at-tawaabil
spinach السبانخ as-sabaanikh
spine العمود الفقري al-'amuud al-fiqrii
spiral لولبي lawlabii
spirits, hard liquor كحول kuhuul
spoiled (does not work) مدلل mudallal
spoiled (of food) فاسد faasid
spoon ملعقة mil'aqa
sponge اسفنج 'isfanj
sports رياضة riyaada
spotted (pattern) منقط munaqqat
spray رشاش rashaash
spring (season) ربيع rabii'
spring (of water) ينبوع yunbuu'
spring (metal part) زنبرك zunbarak
spouse زوج zawj
square (shape) مربع murabba'
square, town square ساحة المدينة saahat al-madiina
squid الحبار al-habbar
staff مساعد musaa'id
stain وقعة waq'a
stairs درج daraj
stall (of vendor) كشك kushk
stall, to (car) يوقف yuuqif
stamp (ink) يختم yakhtim
stamp (postage) طابع taabi'
stand, to يقف yaqif
stand up, to يقف yaqif
star نجمة najma
start, beginning بداية bidaaya
start, to يبدا yabda'
stationery القرطاسية al-qirtaasiyya
statue تمثال timthaal
stay, remain يبقى yabqaa

stay overnight, to يبيت yabiit
steal, to يسرق yasriq
steam بخار bukhaar
steamed مبخر mubakhkhar
steel الفولاذ al-fuulaadh
steer, to يوجه yuwajjih
step خطوة khutwa
steps, stairs درج daraj
stick, pole عصا 'asaa
stick out, to يبرز yabruz
stick to, to يواصل yuwaasil
sticky دبق dabiq
sticky rice أرز دبق aruz dabiq
stiff صلب sulb
still, quiet صامت saamit
still, even now حتى hatta al-'aan
stink, to ينتن yantun
stomach, belly معدة ma'ida
stone حجر hajar
stool كرسي بلا ظهر kursii bilaa zahir
stop (bus, train) محطة mahatta
stop, to halt يوقف yuuqif
stop, to cease يتوقف yatawaqqaf
stop by, to pay a visit يزور yazuur
stop it! توقف tawaqqaf
store, shop متجر matjar
store, to يخزن yakhzin
storey (of a building) طابق taabaq
storm عاصفة 'aasifa
story (tale) قصة qissa
stout شجاع shujaa'
stove, cooker موقد mawqid
straight (not crooked) مستقيم mustaqiim
straight ahead مباشرة mubaasharatan
strait صارم saarim
strange غريب ghariib
stranger أجنبي 'ajnabii
street شارع shaari'
strength قوة quwwa
strict صارم saarim
strike, to go on يذهب yadhhab
strike, hit ضربة darba
string خيط khayt
striped مخطط mukhattat
strong قوي qawii
stubborn, determined عنيد 'aniid
stuck, won't move يتعطل yata'attal
student تلميذ tilmiidh
study, learn يتعلم yata'allam
stupid غبي ghabii
style زي zayy
succeed, to ينجح yanjah
success نجاح najaah
such مثل mithl
such as, for example مثلا mathalan
suck, to يمص yamuss
suddenly فجأة faj'atan
suffer, to يتعذب yata'adhdhab
suffering ألم 'alam
sugar سكر sukkar
sugarcane قصب سكر qasab sukkar
suggest, to يقترح yaqtarih
suggestion اقتراح 'iqtiraah
suit, business طقم taqm
suitable, fitting, compatible ملائم mulaa'im
suitcase حقيبة haqiiba
summer صيف sayf
summit, peak قمة qimma
sun شمس shams
Sunday الأحد al'ahad
sunlight ضوء الشمس daw' ash-shams
sunny مشمس mushmis

sunrise شروق shuruuq
sunset غروب ghuruub
supermarket السوق المركزية as-suuq al-markaziyya
suppose, to يفترض yaftarid
sure أكيد 'akiid
surf امواج متكسرة amwaaj mutakassira
surface سطح sath
surface mail بريد سطحي bariid sathii
surname اللقب al-laqab
surprised مندهش mundahish
surprising مدهش mudhish
surroundings محيط muhiit
survive, to ينجو yanjuu
suspect, to يشك yashukk
suspicion شك shakk
swallow, to يبتلع yabtali'
sweat عرق 'araq
sweat, to يعرق ya'raq
sweep, to يحصد yahsud
sweet حلو hulw
sweet, dessert حلوى halwa
sweet and sour حلو و حامض hulw wa haamid
sweetcorn الذرة السكرية adh-dhura as-sukkariyya
sweets, candy حلوى halwa
swim, to يسبح yasbah
swimming costume, swimsuit ثوب السباحة thawb as-sibaaha
swimming pool مسبح masbah
swing, to يهز yahuzz
switch المفتاح الكهربائي al-miftaah al-kahrabaa'ii
switch, to change يبدل yubaddil
switch on, turn on يشعل yush'il
synthetic إصطناعي istinaa'ii

T

table طاولة taawila
tablecloth غطاء الطاولة ghitaa' at-taawila
tablemat غطا المائدة ghitaa' al-maa'ida
tablets أقراص aqraas
Tagalog التاغالوغي at-taaghaaluughiy
tail ذيل dhayl
take, to remove يأخذ ya'khudh
take care of, to يرعى yar'a
take off (clothes) يخلع yakhla'
talk, to يتكلم yatakallam
talk about يتكلم عن yatakallam 'an
tall طويل tawiil
tame أليف 'aliif
Taoism الطاوية at-taawiyya
tape, adhesive شريط لاصق shariit laasiq
tape recording شريط shariit
taste طعم ta'm
taste, to (sample) يجرب yujarrib
taste, to (salty, spicy) يتذوق yatadhawwaq
tasty لذيذ ladhiidh
taxi سيارة أجرة sayyaarat 'ujraa
tea شاي shaay
teach, to يعلم yu'allim
teacher معلم mu'allim
team فريق fariiq
tear, to rip يمزق yumazziq
tears دموع dumuu'
teenager مراهق muraahiq
teeshirt قميص تائي qamiis taa'iy
teeth أسنان asnaan
telephone هاتف haatif
telephone number رقم الهاتف raqam l-haatif
television تلفز tilfaaz
tell, to (a story) يقص yaquss

tell, to (let know) يخبر yukhbir
temperature حرارة haraara
temple (ancient) بناء قديم binaa' qadiim
temple (Balinese-Hindu) هيكل haykal
temple (Chinese) معبد صيني ma'bad siiniy
temple (Indian) معبد هندي ma'bad hindiy
temporary مؤقت mu'aqqat
ten عشرة 'ashara
tendon وتر watar
tennis كرة المضرب kurat al-madrib
tens of, multiples of ten عشرات 'asharaat
tense متوتر mutawattir
ten thousand عشرة الاف 'asharat 'aalaaf
terrible رهيب rahiib
test اختبار 'ikhtibaar
test, to يختبر yakhtabir
testicles خصيات khusyaat
than من min
Thai تايلندي taylandii
Thailand تايلندا taylandaa
thank, to يشكر yashkur
thankyou شكرا shukran
that (introducing a quotation) ذلك dhaalik
that, those ذلك، اولئك dhaalika, uula'ika
that, which, the one who الذي al-ladhi
theatre (drama) مسرح masrah
their, theirs لهم lahum
then ثم thumma
there هناك hunaaka
therefore لذلك lidhaalik
there is, there are هناك hunaaka
they, them هم hum
thick (of liquids) خاثر khaathir
thick (of things) سميك samiik
thief حرامي haraamii
thigh فخذ fakhidh
thin (of liquids) سائل saa'il
thin (of persons) نحيل nahiil
thing شيء shay'
think, to ponder يفكر yufakkir
think, to have an opinion يظن yazun
third ثالث thaalith
thirsty عطشان 'atshaan
thirteen ثلاثة عشر thalaathata 'ashar
thirty ثلاثين thalaathiin
this, these هذا haadhaa
though مع ذلك ma'a dhaalika
thoughts أفكار 'afkaar
thousand ألف 'alf
thread خيط khayt
threaten, to يهدد yuhaddid
three ثلاثة thalaatha
throat حلق halq
through, past خلال khilaal
throw, to يرمي yarmii
throw away, throw out يبعد yub'id
thunder رعد ra'd
Thursday الخميس al-khamiis
thus, so لذا lidhaa
ticket (for transport) تذكرة tadhkira
ticket (for entertainment) تذكرة tadhkira
tidy مرتب murattab
tidy up يرتب yurattib
tie, necktie ربطة عنق rabtat 'unuq
tie, to يربط yarbit
tiger نمر namir
tight ضيق dayyiq
time وقت waqt

time: from time to time أحيانا ahyaanan

times (multiplying) أوقات 'awqaat

timetable جدول مواعيد jadwal mawaa'iid

tiny صغير saghiir

tip (end) طرف taraf

tip (gratuity) بقشيش baqshiish

tired (sleepy) نعسان na'saan

tired (worn out) متعب mut'ab

title (of book, film) عنوان 'unwaan

title (of person) لقب laqab

to, toward (a person) نحو nahwa

to, toward (a place) الى 'ila

today اليوم al-yawn

toe اصبع القدم 'isba' al-qadam

tofu التوفو at-tuufuu

together معا ma'an

toilet حمام hammaam

tomato طماطم tamaatim

tomorrow غدا ghadan

tongue لسان lisaan

tonight هذه الليلة haadhihi al-layla

too (also) أيضا 'aydan

too (excessive) أكثر من اللازم akthar mina l-laazim

too much كثيرا kathiiran

tool, utensil, instrument آلة aala

tooth سن sinn

toothbrush فرشاة أسنان furshaat asnaan

toothpaste معجون أسنان ma'juun 'asnaan

top قمة qimma

topic موضوع mawduu'

torch, flashlight مشعل mish'al

total مجموع majmuu'

touch, to يلمس yalmas

tourist سائح saa'ih

toward قريب qariib

towel منشفة minshafa

tower برج burj

town قرية qarya

toy لعبة lu'ba

trade, business تجارة tijaara

trade, to exchange يتبادل yatabaadal

traditional تقليدي taqliidii

traffic المرور al-muruur

train قطار qitaar

train station محطة القطار mahattat al-qitaar

training تمرين tamriin

translate, to يترجم yutarjim

travel, to يسافر yusaafir

traveller مسافر musaafir

tray صينية sayniyya

treat (something special) متعة mut'a

treat, to (behave towards) يعامل yu'aamil

treat, to (medically) يعالج yu'aalij

tree شجرة shajara

triangle مثلث muthallath

tribe قبيلة qabiila

trip, journey رحلة rihla

troops جيوش juyuush

trouble مشكلة mushkila

troublesome مزعج muz'ij

trousers بنطلون bantaluun

truck شاحنة shaahina

true صحيح sahiih

truly بإخلاص bi'ikhlaas

trust, to يثق yathiq

try, to يجرب yujarrib

try on (clothes) يقيس yaqiis

Tuesday الثلاثاء ath-thulaathaa'

turn, make a turn ينعطف yan'atif
turn around, to يدور yaduur
turn off, to يطفئ yutfi'
turn on, to يشعل yush'il
turtle (land) سلحفاة sulahfaat
turtle (sea) سلحفاة البحر sulahfaat l-bahr
TV تلفاز tilfaaz
twelve اثني عشر 'ithnay 'ashar
twenty عشرين 'ishriin
two اثنين 'ithnayn
type, sort نوع naw'
type, to يطبع yatba'
typhoon اعصار استوائي 'i'saar 'istiwaa'i
typical نموذجي namuudhajii

U

ugly بشع bashi'
umbrella مظلة mizalla
uncle عم 'amm
uncooked نيء nayyi'
under تحت tahta
undergo, to يخضع yakhda'
underpants ثياب داخلية thiyaab daakhiliyya
undershirt قميص داخلي qamiis daakhilii
understand, to يفهم yafham
underwear ثياب داخلية thiyaab daakhiliyya
undressed, to get يتعرى yata'arra
unfortunately للاسف lil'asaf
unemployed عاطل عن العمل 'aatil 'an al-'amal
unhappy حزين haziin
United Kingdom بريطانيا bariitaaniya
United States الولايات المتحدة الأمريكية al-wilaayaat al-muttahida al-'amriikiyya
university جامعة jaami'a
unless الا اذا 'illaa 'idhaa
unlucky تعيس الحظ ta'iis al-haz
unnecessary غير ضروري ghayr daruurii
unripe فج fijj
until حتى hatta
up, upward فوق fawqa
upset, unhappy حزين haziin
upside down رأسا على عقب ra'san 'ala 'aqib
upstairs في الأعلى fi l-a'laa
urban مدني madanii
urge, to push for يحث yahuth
urgent ملح mulihh
urinate, to يتبول yatabawwal
use, to يستعمل yasta'mil
used to, accustomed متعود muta'awwid
used to do something متعود muta'awwid
useful مفيد mufiid
useless عديم الجدوى 'adiim al-jadwaa
usual معتاد mu'taad
usually عادة 'aadatan
uterus الرحم ar-rahim

V

vacation عطلة 'utla
vaccination تطعيم tat'iim
vagina مهبل mahbil
vague غامض ghaamid
valid شرعي shar'ii
valley وادي waadii
value (cost) سعر si'ir
value, good قيمة qiima
value, to يقدر yuqaddir
vase مزهرية mazhariyya
VCR جهاز الفيديو jihaaz l-fiidyuu
vegetable نبات nabaat
vegetables خضار khudaar

W

ENGLISH–ARABIC

vehicle سيارة sayyaara
very, extremely كثيرا kathiiran
vest, undershirt صدرة sudra
via عبر 'abra
video cassette شريط تلفزيوني sharrit tilfizyuunii
video recorder الكاميرا al-kaamira
videotape, to يسجل yusajjil
Vietnam الفيتنام al-fiyitnaam
Vietnamese اللغة الفيتنامية al-lugha al-fiyitnaamiyya
view, panorama مشهد mashhad
view, look at يشاهد yushaahid
village قرية qarya
vinegar خل khal
visa تأشير ta'shiira
visit زيارة ziyaara
visit, to pay a يزور yazuur
voice صوت sawt
voicemail جهاز الرد الآلي jihaaz ar-radd al-'aaliy
volcano بركان burkaan
vomit, to يتقيأ yataqayya'
vote, to ينتخب yantakhib

W

wages راتب raatib
wait for, to ينتظر yantazir
waiter, waitress نادل naadil
wake up يستيقظ yastayqiz
wake someone up يوقظ yuuqiz
Wales بلاد الغال bilad al-ghaal
walk, to يمشي yamshii
walking distance مسافة مشي masaafat mashyin
wall حائط haa'it
wallet محفظة mihfaza
want, to يريد yuriid
war حرب harb
war, to make يحارب yuhaarib
warm دافئ daafi'
warmth دفء dif'
warn, to ينبه yunabbih
warning تنبيه tanbiih
wash, to يغسل yaghsil
wash the dishes يغسل الصحون yaghsil as-suhuun
watch (wristwatch) ساعة يدوية saa'a yadawiyya
watch, to (show, movie) يشاهد yushaahid
watch, look, see يشاهد yushaahid
watch over, guard يحرس yahrus
water ماء maa'
water buffalo جاموس الماء jaamuus al-maa'
waterfall شلال shallaal
watermelon بطيخ battiikh
wave (in sea) موجة mawja
wave, to يلوح yulawwih
wax شمع sham'a
way, method طريقة tariiqa
way: by way of عن طريق 'an tariiq
way in مدخل madkhal
way out محرج makhraj
we, us (excludes the one addressed) نحن nahnu
we, us (includes the one addressed) نحن nahnu
weak ضعيف da'iif
wealthy غني ghanii
weapon سلاح silaah
wear, to يرتدي yartadii
weary مرهق murhaq
weather طقس taqs
weave, to ينسج yansij
weaving ينسج nasiij
website موقع الانترنيت mawqi' al'antirniit
wedding زفاف zifaaf
Wednesday الأربعاء al-'arbi'aa'
week أسبوع 'usbuu'

weekend عطلة نهاية الأسبوع ’utlat nihaayat al-usbuu’
weekly أسبوعيا ’usbuu’iyyan
weep, to يبكي yabkii
weigh, to يزن yazin
weigh out, to يزن yazin
weight وزن wazn
weight, to gain يسمن yasman
weight, to lose يضعف yad’uf
welcome! أهلا و سهلا ’ahlan wa sahlan
welcome, to يرحب yurahhib
well, good جيد jayyid
well (for water) بئر bi’r
well-behaved حسن السلوك hasan as-suluuk
well-cooked, well-done مطهو جيدا mathuu jayyidan
well done! أحسنت ’ahsanta
well-mannered مهذب muhadhdhab
well off, wealthy غني ghanii
Welsh لغة بلاد الغال lughat bilaad al-ghaal
west غرب gharb
westerner غربي gharbii
wet مبلل muballal
what? ماذا maadhaa
what for? لماذا limaadhaa
what kind of? أي نوع ’ay naw’
what time? أي وقت ’ay waqt
wheel دولاب dulaab
when? متى mataa
when, at the time عندما ’indamaa
whenever كلما kullamaa
where? أين ’ayn
where to? الى أين ’ila ’ayn
which? أي ’ay
while, during خلال khilaal
white أبيض ’abyad
who? من man
whole, all of كل kul
whole, to be complete كامل kaamil
why? لماذا limaadha
wicked شرير shirriir
wide عريض ’ariid
width عرض ’ard
widow أرملة ’armala
widowed أرملة ’armala
widower أرمل ’armal
wife زوجة zawja
wild شرس sharis
will, shall سوف sawfa
win, to يربح yarbah
wind, breeze نسيم nasiim
window (in house) نافذة naafidha
window (for paying, buying tickets) شباك التذاكر shubbaak at-tadhaakir
wine نبيذ nabiidh
wing جناح janaah
winner فائز faa’iz
winter شتاء shitaa’
wipe, to يمسح yamsah
wire سلك silk
wise حكيم hakiim
wish, to يتمنى yatamanna
with مع ma’a
within reason معقول ma’quul
without بدون biduun
witness شاهد shaahid
witness, to يشهد yashhad
woman امرأة ’imra’a
wonderful رائع raa’i’
wood خشب khashab
wooden خشبي khashabii
wool صوف suuf
word كلمة kalima
work, occupation مهنة mihna
work, to يعمل ya’mal
work, to function يعمل ya’mal

Y

world العالم al-'aalam
worn out, tired متعب mut'ab
worn out (clothes, machine) قديم qadiim
worry, to يقلق yaqlaq
worse أسوأ 'aswa'
worship, to يعبد ya'bud
worst الأسوأ al-'aswa'
worth, to be ذو قيمة <u>th</u>uu qiima
wound جرح jur<u>h</u>
wrap, to يغلف yu<u>gh</u>allif
wrist معصم mi'<u>s</u>am
write, to يكتب yaktub
writer كاتب kaatib
wrong (false) خطأ <u>kh</u>a<u>t</u>a'
wrong (mistaken) مخطئ mu<u>kh</u>ti'
wrong (morally) باطل baa<u>t</u>il

Y

yawn تثاؤب ta<u>th</u>aa'ub
year سنة sana
years old سن sinn

yell, to يصرخ ya<u>s</u>ru<u>kh</u>
yellow أصفر 'a<u>s</u>far
yes نعم na'am
yesterday البارحة al-baari<u>h</u>a
yet: not yet بعد ba'd
you (familiar) أنت 'anta
you (female) أنت 'anti
you (male) أنت 'anta
you're welcome! العفو al-'afw
Young شاب <u>sh</u>aab
younger brother or sister أصغر 'a<u>s</u>ghar
youth (state of being young) شباب <u>sh</u>abaab
youth (young person) شاب <u>sh</u>aab

Z

zero صفر <u>s</u>ifr
zoo حديقة الحيوانات <u>h</u>adiiqat al-<u>h</u>ayawaanaat
zucchini, courgettes كوسا kuusaa